LEADERS OF THE CIVIL WAR ERA

Abraham Lincoln

LEADERS OF THE CIVIL WAR ERA

John Brown

Jefferson Davis

Frederick Douglass

Ulysses S. Grant

Stonewall Jackson

Robert E. Lee

Abraham Lincoln

William Tecumseh Sherman

Harriet Beecher Stowe

Harriet Tubman

LEADERS OF THE CIVIL WAR ERA

Abraham Lincoln

Rachel A. Koestler-Grack

CHELSEA HOUSE
PUBLISHERS
An imprint of Infobase Publishing

ABRAHAM LINCOLN

Copyright ©2009 by Infobase Publishing

Chelsea House
An imprint of Infobase Publishing
132 West 31st Street
New York NY 10001

Library of Congress Cataloging-in-Publication Data
Koestler-Grack, Rachel A., 1973–
Abraham Lincoln / Rachel Koestler-Grack.
     p. cm. — (Leaders of the Civil War era)
Includes bibliographical references and index.
ISBN 978-1-60413-298-4 (hardcover : acid-free paper)
1. Lincoln, Abraham, 1809–1865—Juvenile literature. 2. Presidents—United States—
Biography—Juvenile literature. 3. United States--History—Civil War, 1861–1865—Juvenile
literature. I. Title. II. Series.
E457.905.K54 2009
973.7092—dc22
[B]   2008043030

Chelsea House books are available at special discounts when purchased in bulk quantities
for businesses, associations, institutions, or sales promotions. Please call our Special Sales
Department in New York at (212) 967-8800 or (800) 322-8755.

You can find Chelsea House on the World Wide Web at http://www.chelseahouse.com

Series design by Erik Lindstrom
Cover design by Keith Trego

Printed in the United States of America

Bang KT 10 9 8 7 6 5 4 3 2 1

This book is printed on acid-free paper.

All links and Web addresses were checked and verified to be correct at the time of
publication. Because of the dynamic nature of the Web, some addresses and links may have
changed since publication and may no longer be valid.

⚔ CONTENTS ⚔

Forever Free

On January 1, 1863, President Abraham Lincoln signed into effect one of the most controversial and contested documents in American history—the Emancipation Proclamation. After three years of bloody Civil War, Lincoln declared that "all persons held as slaves within any State or designated part of a State, the people whereof shall then be in rebellion against the United States, shall be then, thenceforward, and forever free." Lincoln's bold proclamation abolished slavery within the rebellious states of the Confederacy and brought hope of future freedom to still-enslaved African Americans in the slaveholding states that had remained loyal to the Union. The proclamation also changed the course of American history forever.

Although the Emancipation Proclamation eventually led to the fall of slavery in the United States, it did not immediately free a single slave. Freedom depended on a Union victory. The proclamation completely transformed the character of the war, however. Up until this time, the war had not been about freeing slaves. For Lincoln, the Civil War was fought to preserve the Union. Slavery was a key issue and hotly debated, but it was just one of the factors that had led to the conflict.

Besides holding differing views on slavery, America's Northern and Southern states had very different economies. The economies of the Northern states were based on businesses, factories, and small farms. In the South, the regional economy depended heavily on plantations where cotton, tobacco, rice, and sugarcane were grown in vast fields. Plantation owners relied on slaves to work their fields. Without slave labor, the Southern economy would crumble.

In the early 1800s, the issue of slavery began to heat up. Believing that slavery was cruel and immoral, many Northern states had outlawed the practice. Some abolitionists—people who spoke out against slavery and worked to end it—thought that slavery should be illegal in all states. Southerners resented this perceived interference in their way of life, and tempers flared. Wealthy plantation owners, many of whom were also politicians, vehemently opposed such a suggestion. The North and South also disagreed about the role of government. Southerners believed that each state should have the right to make its own laws regarding social issues, including slavery. People in the North, on the other hand, favored a strong national government. In the view of most Northerners, the federal government should have the power to make both political and social decisions for the entire country.

By 1860, the conflict between North and South had come to a full boil. In that year's presidential election, Republican candidate Abraham Lincoln—fresh from the Midwestern prairie—favored a strong federal government and opposed the expansion of slavery in the United States. At a time when the nation was expanding westward, Lincoln believed that slavery

Slavery in the United States began in 1619 when the Dutch ship the *White Lion* came ashore with 20 enslaved Africans at Old Point Comfort, the site of present-day Fort Monroe in Virginia. Eventually, the slave population grew to 4 million by the 1860 census and slavery lasted until the passage of the Thirteenth Amendment in 1865. In this picture, a white landowner oversees black slaves picking cotton in Texas.

should not be allowed to spread into new states and territories. At the same time, he never called for an end of slavery in current slave states. Nevertheless, Southerners felt threatened. If new territories joined the Union as free states, the slave states soon would be outnumbered. Moreover, if the federal government had the right to decide whether a state would be free or slave, before long, Southern representatives in Congress would not have an equal say.

When Lincoln won the election, seven Southern states immediately withdrew, or seceded, from the Union. The rebellious states formed a new government and established their own country—the Confederate States of America. By 1861, four more states had joined the Confederacy. Lincoln wanted the Union to stay together, and refused to acknowledge the Confederate States of America as a separate country. It was too late to win back the South, however; the Rebels had made up their minds. On April 12, 1861, Confederate troops opened fire on Union troops at Fort Sumter in South Carolina. The Civil War had begun.

SLAVERY: LINCOLN'S HOT POTATO

In the beginning, President Lincoln remained cautious in dealing with the issue of slavery. He wanted to maintain the loyalty of the border states where slavery was still legal. After the outbreak of the Civil War, however, slaves began to flee to Union Army lines to claim their freedom. With increasing numbers of slaves escaping to Northern states, the issue became nearly impossible to avoid. People in the North urged Lincoln to free all slaves. Still, Lincoln dragged his feet. Congress had been tossing around the issue of slavery like a hot potato. Deep down, Lincoln hoped to convince the Southern states to return to the Union. If he freed all slaves, there would be no hope of reconciliation. As the war dragged on, however, Lincoln realized that the states of the Confederacy would rather fight to the death than rejoin the Union.

For the first 18 months of the war, the legal status of African-American slaves remained uncertain. On August 6, 1861, Congress passed the Confiscation Bill, which granted soldiers the right to seize all property—including slaves—that could be used in the rebellion. In September 1862, after the Union victory at Antietam, Lincoln issued a preliminary proclamation freeing all slaves in the rebellious states. This first proclamation, like the final one that followed in 1863, did not apply to the loyal border states—Kentucky, Missouri, Delaware, Maryland, and West Virginia—or to any Southern state already under Union control. In fact, it was not until the passage of the Thirteenth Amendment to the Constitution in 1865 that slavery was completely abolished throughout the United States.

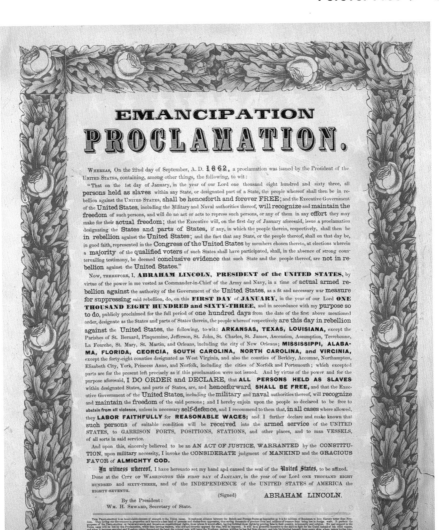

President Abraham Lincoln issued the Emancipation Proclamation on January 1, 1863, as the nation approached its third year of the Civil War. Although it changed the character of the war, it was limited in many ways. It applied only to states that had seceded from the Union, leaving slavery intact in the border states. Also the freedom it promised depended upon Union military victory, which was not assured.

Nevertheless, in 1863, the effects of the Emancipation Proclamation were astounding. The proclamation robbed the Confederacy of the slave labor it had been using in its war effort. This further battered an already weakening Confederate Army. The proclamation also freed African Americans to fight for the Union, thereby giving an extra boost to the Union Army. By the end of the war, in 1865, about 186,000 African-American men had fought on the Union side. After the proclamation, there also was a shift in the way the world viewed the war. People began to look at the war in terms of slavery: The proslavery Confederacy was pitted against the antislavery Union. Because of antislavery sentiment in France and Great Britain, the Confederacy's hopes of gaining or maintaining foreign support were shattered. Although the Emancipation Proclamation played a major role in military strategy, its ultimate result, freedom for all, had a much greater impact on the future.

Abraham Lincoln had grown up in the wilderness of the American frontier. He possessed the strength, the endurance, and the perseverance to carry his nation through the most tumultuous era in its history. Tragically, however, President Lincoln was assassinated just days after the Civil War's end. He never got the chance to see his country heal and to help mend a war-torn land. At least he died knowing that the Union had been brought back together.

Bluegrass Beginnings

O n Sunday, February 12, 1809, the sun rose into a cloud-less, crystal sky over the frosted waters of Nolin Creek. The sun's beams did little, however, to warm the crisp breeze that swirled outside the cabin of Thomas and Nancy Lincoln. Inside, safe and snug from the winter winds, Nancy gently rocked her newborn baby, Abraham. On the floor beside her, two-year-old Sarah played on a fuzzy bearskin rug.

Thirty-three years earlier, in 1776, the thirteen American colonies had delivered their famous Declaration of Independence to Great Britain. That same year, Samuel Lincoln, a captain in the militia, was busy working his 210-acre farm in Rockingham County, Virginia. Samuel Lincoln, the son of an English immigrant, was the grandfather to the sixteenth president of the future United States. Like many English, Scottish, Irish,

German, and Dutch immigrants, Lincoln's family had settled on the grassy slopes of the Shenandoah Valley. Samuel married Bathsheba Herring, and eventually, the family grew to seven. They had three sons—Mordecai, Josiah, and Thomas—and two daughters—Mary and Nancy.

On occasion, Samuel's friend, explorer and backwoodsman Daniel Boone, dropped by for a visit. He rambled on for hours with incredible tales about a wild and beautiful frontier. The lush valleys of Kentucky, he said, were rich with black soil and towering timber. At that time, land in the unsettled region of Kentucky could be purchased for 40 cents per acre. Finally, after hearing one too many stories, Samuel decided to invest in an adventure of his own. Lincoln sold his farm, packed up his family's belongings, and joined a traveling party that was heading out on the Wilderness Road, through the Cumberland Gap, and north and west into the fringes of Kentucky's bluegrass country. The Lincolns settled at last on a vast tract of land, more than 2,000 acres, near the Green River.

In the late 1700s, the Kentucky frontier was hostile country. American Indians were unhappy that white settlers were moving into their territories and forcing them off of their native land. At times, groups of angry American Indians raided pioneer settlements. One afternoon in 1786, Samuel Lincoln and his sons went out to work in their field. Suddenly, a rifle shot rang out from the nearby woods. Lincoln collapsed, shot and killed by the bullet. The three boys spotted American Indians in the trees. Immediately, Mordecai ran to a nearby cabin, and Josiah sprinted toward the local fort to get help. Six-year-old Thomas, or Tom, shocked and terrified, stood staring at his father's bloody body, unable to move. When he looked up, his eyes met those of an American Indian who was standing over him. A shiny medallion hung over the man's left shoulder, near his heart. The next thing Tom heard was the whine of a bullet as it whizzed past his ear. In an instant, the American Indian clenched his chest and crumpled to the ground. Through a crack in the window of the cabin, young Mordecai had taken careful aim at the man's shimmering medallion. With one crucial shot, he killed the man and saved his brother.

To help earn money for their fatherless family, Tom and his brothers became wandering labor boys. They worked as farm-hands for nearby settlers. Along the way, Thomas learned the trades of carpentry and cabinetmaking. Although he was able to read, he had little interest in books. At age 19, Tom served in the Kentucky state militia. When he was 24, he was appointed a constable in Cumberland County. By 1803, he had saved up enough money to buy a 240-acre piece of land near Mill Creek, seven miles north of Elizabethtown. Three years later, Tom took a job with Bleakley & Montgomery, storekeepers in Elizabethtown. They hired him to take a flatboat of merchandise down the Ohio and Mississippi rivers to New Orleans.

At about this time, Tom met 22-year-old Nancy Hanks, a tall, slender woman with dark hair. Like Tom, Nancy had also traveled through the Cumberland Gap to Kentucky. Tom quickly fell in love and asked Nancy to marry him. On June 12, 1806, 28-year-old Tom waited for his bride-to-be wearing a new black suit, silk suspenders, and a fancy beaver hat. When Nancy appeared, she was a vision of beauty, draped in linen and silk. Around her waist, she wore the scarlet sash that Tom had bought for her in Bleakley & Montgomery's store. The couple was married in a lovely ceremony in the little settlement of Beechland, in Washington County, surrounded by family and friends. After a reception feast and a dance to fiddle music, the newlyweds rode away on horseback, down the red-clay roads of the timber trails to Elizabethtown. Their first home was a small cabin near the county courthouse. Soon after the wedding, Tom started work as a carpenter. He built cabinets, doors, window frames, and an occasional coffin.

On February 10, 1807, Tom and Nancy welcomed their first child—little Sarah. The following year, Tom bought Sinking

Spring Farm, on the south fork of Nolin Creek, 18 miles southeast of Elizabethtown. With this purchase, Tom owned a total of 586 acres of land, as well as two lots in Elizabethtown and some livestock. Tom built a one-room log cabin out of timber from his new land and moved his family to Nolin Creek. The cabin had a packed dirt floor, one door, a single small window, and a broad fireplace. Here, on February 12, 1809, Nancy gave birth to Abraham.

In the spring of 1811, Tom once again moved his family, this time 10 miles northeast to a 230-acre farm that he had bought on Knob Creek. It was of this house that Abraham Lincoln had his earliest memories, at about age three. From the yard, little Abe watched covered wagons wobble along the Cumberland Trail. Even as a young child, Abe was expected to help with household chores. He hauled buckets of water from the creek, filled the firewood box, and cleaned the ashes from the fireplace. He also helped in the fields; he hoed and planted rows of beans, onions, corn, and potatoes.

In 1812, young Abe and Sarah anxiously awaited the arrival of a baby sister or brother. Finally the day came, and Nancy gave birth to another boy. He was named Thomas, after his father. A few days later, however, the baby died. He was buried in a tiny coffin that his father made.

While he lived on Knob Creek, Abe had his first experience with school. At that time, most rural schools held classes only when children were not needed to help on the farms. When school was is session, Sarah and Abe walked a mile and a half to a log schoolhouse with a dirt floor. They sat on backless wooden benches as they learned to read and write. The school that Abe attended was called a "blab school." Before reciting their lessons to the teacher, the students read aloud to themselves so that the teacher knew they were studying.

When classes ended, young Abe spent a good part of the day playing with friends. One day, Abe and an older boy named Austin Gollaher decided to cross the creek to hunt

Pictured is the log cabin where Abraham Lincoln was born on February 12, 1809, in Hardin County, Kentucky. Lincoln was the first president born outside of the Thirteen Colonies.

some partridges that Abe had seen the day before. Recent rains had caused the creek to swell, pushing water up the banks and quickening the current. The only bridge across the creek was a narrow log. Abe had got about halfway across when his foot slipped. He plunged into the creek. Neither Abe nor Austin knew how to swim. Austin grabbed a long branch and held it out to Abe. Abe managed to grasp it, and Austin pulled him to shore. As Austin dragged Abe out of the water, however, the younger boy collapsed. Working fast, Austin rolled him over and pounded his chest. Abe would not wake up. Austin then pulled Abe onto his feet and shook him until water drained out of his mouth. Finally, with a fit of coughing, Abe came to.

As soon as Abe calmed down, the two boys began to worry about getting into trouble. Surely, if they came home soaking wet, their mothers would give them a good whipping. They decided to lay their sopping clothes on some rocks to let the warm June sun dry them. As the boys stood along the bank of Knob Creek in their underwear, waiting for the clothes to dry, they vowed never to tell anyone about what had happened that day.

Tom and Nancy taught their children to be gentle, kind, generous, and patriotic. In later years, Abraham Lincoln could not recall much about the War of 1812. His sole memory was of a day when, on his way home from fishing, he met a soldier. Abe was carrying his catch, a single, small fish. His mother always had told him to be kind to soldiers. Young Abe gave the man his fish.

"PINCHING TIMES"

In December 1816, the Lincoln family made another move. They waved good-bye to Kentucky and by horseback and covered wagon headed north through wild, untamed country. They crossed the Ohio River and entered Indiana. At times, the bushes and vines along their way were so entangled and so thick that Tom had to hack out a trail with his ax. It was a frightening adventure for young Abe. As quoted by biographer Carl Sandburg, in *Abraham Lincoln: the Prairie Years and the War Years*, Lincoln later wrote, "It was a wild region, with many bears and other wild animals still in the woods." Lincoln went on: "The panther's scream filled the night with fear, [and] bears preyed on the swine." Finally, 16 miles from the Ohio River, on a spot that today is Lincoln City, the family built a crude pole shed in a clearing near Little Pigeon Creek. During the winter weeks that followed, Tom built an 18-foot-by-20-foot cabin with a loft.

When Abe was seven years old, he had his first experience with hunting. It was an incident he never forgot. Standing inside his new log cabin, young Abe watched a flock of wild turkeys strut toward the house. He slowly slid his rifle through a crack in the window and pulled the trigger. The shot killed one of the birds. He was so struck with remorse for killing the innocent creature that he vowed never to hunt again. He simply did not like shooting to kill.

That first year in Indiana brought hard, "pinching times," as Lincoln later called them. The family worked day after day to chop down trees and clear away underbrush. On the Indiana frontier, the soil had never been worked and turned to prepare it for planting crops. The family put in long, backbreaking hours plowing up the unbroken ground. Without access to stores or markets, all of their food had to come from the wilderness around them. Tom hunted deer, bear, wild turkeys, ducks, and geese. Abe and Sarah gathered nuts and wild fruits from the woods. Although Tom dug several wells, they all went dry. The children had to walk nearly a mile each way to fetch water from a spring.

In the fall of 1818, Nancy noticed a white residue on her tongue. Her stomach cramped and burned. She knew all too well what these symptoms meant. She was infected with "milk sickness," a fatal illness caused by drinking milk from cows that had eaten poisonous snakeroot plants. Just months earlier, another couple—friends of the Lincolns who also had moved to Indiana from Kentucky—had come down with the sickness and died. Nancy and Tom had taken their friends' son, Dennis, into their home. When Nancy felt death approaching, she called her children to her bedside. She placed her feeble hand on little Abe's head and told him to be good to his father and sister. Within one short week of discovering her infection, on October 5, 1818, Nancy died. She was just 34 years old. Twelve-year-old Sarah took over as housekeeper and cook, and nine-year-old Abe continued to work with his father in the fields.

Tom knew that he needed a mother for his children. He decided to make the long journey back to Elizabethtown, Kentucky, to propose to a widow there, Sarah Bush Johnston. When he arrived at her house, he got right to the point. "I have no wife and you no husband. I came a-purpose to marry you," he said. Sarah accepted his proposal. They were married on December 2, 1819. Sarah had three children from her first marriage: 13-year-old Sarah Elizabeth, 10-year-old Matilda, and 9-year-old John D. Johnston. When Sarah and her children arrived at their new home in Indiana, the whole family had to get used to the tight living space. Abe did not seem to mind. He immediately felt the warm affection of his stepmother and was comforted by her rosy cheeks and kind eyes. In time, he grew to love her.

When she first arrived in Indiana, Sarah must have been a bit surprised at what she found: a windowless, dirt-floored cabin and dirty children dressed in rags. Almost at once, the house took on a whole new character. Sarah gave Abe and little Sarah a good scrubbing and dressed them in nice clothes. Tom went right to work to saw lumber for a new wood-plank floor. Before long, the house was warm and happy.

BRAINS AND BRAWN

When Abe was 11, he went back to school—at least, that is, he did so when a teacher happened to wander through the Indiana countryside. The little local schoolhouse sat quiet and empty until a roaming schoolteacher moved in, usually during the winter. As soon as spring planting rolled around, the school-master generally disappeared and classes abruptly ended. Because of these conditions, Abe's entire schooling amounted to less than a year. The nearest schoolhouse was four miles from the Lincolns' cabin—a long, cold walk in the winter.

In Kentucky, at Sinking Spring Farm, the schoolteachers had used only spelling books to teach the children to read. In those days, pupils memorized the spelling book several times before they began reading. Abe knew how to spell "incomprehensibility"—an eight-syllable word—before he could read the sentence "Ann can spin flax." He had studied Noah Webster's so-called "blue-back speller." In Indiana, he

Rural life was harsh and there was very little time for play or schooling. Often teachers were barely more educated than their students. Most families did not own books besides the Bible. Although Lincoln only had 18 months of formal schooling, he learned to read, write, and do math at an early age. Lincoln was often found with a book in his hands and was punished many times for neglecting his farm work.

now graduated to Lindley Murray's *English Reader*, which he believed was the best book an American boy could read.

Once he had learned how to read, Abe became a bookworm. He carried a book with him everywhere he went and read almost every chance he got. On workdays, he stuffed a book in his shirt, jammed corn dodgers—corn-bread cakes—in his pocket, and headed out to plow or hoe. When noon rolled around, he sat down under a good shade tree, pulled out his book, and ate as he read. At night, he pulled a chair close to the fire and read some more. When his siblings teased him, his stepmother, Sarah, told the children to leave him alone. "Abe is going to be a great man someday," she said, "and I'm not going to have him be hindered." Abe's stepmother constantly encouraged him with his studies. Years later, Abe said, "She has been my best friend in this world."

Abe also said, "The things I want to know are in books. My best friend is the man who'll get me a book I ain't read." One fall afternoon, Abe walked to see a lawyer in Rockport, Indiana, nearly 20 miles away, because he had heard about a book that the lawyer owned. A few days later, Abe husked corn from sunrise to sundown. Then, after supper, he read the book by the fire until midnight. He also read the family Bible, the only book in the Lincoln cabin. Young Abe borrowed and read many other books, however, such as *Aesop's Fables*, John Bunyan's *Pilgrim's Progress*, Daniel Defoe's *Robinson Crusoe*, William Grimshaw's *History of the United States*, and Parson M.L. Weems's *Life of George Washington*.

One night, after reading a few pages in the *Life of Washington*, Abe set the book on a shelf beside his bed. That night, a terrible rainstorm pounded against the cabin. In the morning, Abe noticed that his borrowed book was sopping wet. There was a crack between the logs in the wall just above his shelf, and the strong winds had blown rainwater into the cabin, drenching the book. Taking full responsibility for the damage, he pulled hay for three days to pay for the damaged book.

At school, teachers noticed that Abe was a born leader. He was an excellent speller and a smooth reader, his penmanship was clean and neat, and he had solid writing skills. His essays reflected deep thoughts and opinions on many topics. Always striving for fairness, honesty, and justice, Abe won the respect of his teachers and his friends. He was known as a captivating storyteller, a clever debater, and a fun-loving friend.

During his teenage years, Abe endured an extreme growth spurt. As he shot up, he changed not only in appearance, but also in personality. Physically, the rapid growth in his arms and legs caused him to lose coordination. To compensate, he moved more slowly and carefully. Although still quick-witted and ready with an answer, Abe also slowed down his thinking process. Often, during a conversation, his eyes lost focus as he drifted into deep thoughtfulness and refection.

By the time he turned 17, Abe stood a towering six feet, four inches tall. He had long, muscular arms. His baggy pants usually were several inches too short for his long legs, exposing his bony ankles. Although he was not particularly handsome, he was brave and kind. He attracted the admiration of many young ladies. His unusual strength came in handy for farm work, and he became known for how deeply he could sink an ax into a tree trunk.

One fall, Abe was hired to clear trees from an area of woodland. His youngest stepsister, Matilda, always begged to go along, but her mother, Sarah, did not allow it. One morning, as Abe set out, Matilda sneaked away from the cabin and slipped through the bushes after Abe. Creeping up behind her brother, Matilda took a catlike leap through the air. She landed on Abe's back and knocked him down. As the two tumbled to the ground, Abe's ax gouged into Matilda's ankle. Abe tore a strip of cloth from his shirt and bandaged the wound. After he dried her tears, he sternly asked his disobedient sister, "'Tilda, what are you going to tell mother about getting hurt?"

"I'll tell her I did it with the ax," she sobbed. "That will be the truth, won't it?"

"Yes, that's the truth, 'Tilda," said Abe, "but it's not the whole truth. Tell the whole truth, 'Tilda, and trust your good mother for the rest." It was incidents such as this one that earned Abraham Lincoln the reputation and nickname of "Honest Abe."

The woods of Kentucky and the woods of Indiana were much alike. Indiana had something that Sinking Spring Farm

The family farm in Indiana was near the Ohio River, and as a young man, Lincoln often earned money ferrying passengers and baggage to riverboats waiting midstream *(depicted above)*. He gained recognition for his skill in getting a 40-foot flatboat unstuck in the waters of New Salem, near Springfield, Illinois.

did not, however: the mighty Ohio River. In 1826, Abe took a job with James Taylor, who owned a store on Posey's Landing at the mouth of Anderson Creek. Taylor also operated a ferry across the creek. From the docks, Abe watched steamboats belch puffs of smoke from their stacks as strings of flatboats loaded with cargo lumbered down the river. Abe's job was to ferry passengers from the landing across Anderson Creek.

In the spring of 1827, Abe built a flat-bottomed boat and started doing a little ferrying business of his own on the side. He took passengers from the Indiana shore to steamboats stopped midstream on the Ohio River. In this way, he could earn an extra honest penny or so. Once, two travelers, anxious to catch a steamer, asked Abe to row them out to the boat. When they got to the steamer, Abe lifted their trunks onboard. Each traveler tossed Abe a silver half-dollar. The most Abe had ever earned in one day was 31 cents. As he reached out to catch the coins, one of them slipped through his fingers to disappear beneath the murky ripples in the water.

On the other side of the Ohio River from Abe's ferry business, a man named John Dill operated another ferry. Mr. Dill held the sole license to ferry across the Ohio River from the Kentucky shore to the mouth of Anderson's Creek. When Dill saw Abe doing ferry business in his water, he set out to put an end to it. One day, when Abe was out in his boat, Dill waved him over to the Kentucky shore. As soon as Abe pulled his boat up the bank, Dill's brother jumped out from behind some bushes, and the two Dills grabbed Abe. They accused Abe of stealing their business and threatened to dunk him in the river. After getting a good look at Abe's size, however, they reconsidered. The two men ordered Abe to go with them to the house of a magistrate to have the issue settle by the law. Believing that he had done nothing wrong, Abe agreed. He followed the Dill brothers to the nearby house of Squire Samuel Pate, a local lawyer.

At Pate's house, the Dills filed a formal warrant against Abe. They claimed that he was running a ferry on the Ohio River without a license—a violation of Kentucky law. They explained to the magistrate that Abe had transported passengers from the Indiana shore to steamboats on the Ohio River. The river belonged to Kentucky, and John Dill held the only proper license to ferry on it.

   Pate turned to Abe and asked to hear his side of the story. Abe admitted that he had ferried passengers on the Ohio River. He argued, however, that Dill's license only gave him the exclusive right to ferry between specific points on the Ohio River. It did not forbid others from transporting passengers to the middle of the stream. Abe assured Pate that he had never intended to break any laws and did not think he had done so. After all, he had carried passengers only from the Indiana shore to the middle of the river, never to the Kentucky shore. Pate carefully examined a copy of a book of the statutes of Kentucky, which contained the details of the law in question. Pate then dismissed the charges against Abe because the law applied to anyone taking a passenger across the river, not to the middle of it. The two Dills left Pate's house and dropped the issue forever.

BRUSH WITH DEATH

The main farm crop in Indiana, as in Kentucky, was corn. Many frontier homes had handmills, which families used to grind small amounts of corn for personal use. To grind larger quantities, however, farmers had to take their corn to a public mill. When the streams rushed with water, the mills ran on water power. If rainfall was low, however, and the levels of the streams were down, a farmer who brought corn to a mill had to hitch up his own horse to the stone grinder. The horse had to walk around and around in a circle as the millstones crushed the corn into meal. It was a painfully slow process.

   One day, young Abe Lincoln rode his father's gray mare to Gordon's gristmill, several miles away from home. On

After the ruling, Abe stuck around to chat with Pate. Squire Pate explained that many such disagreements arise because people do not educate themselves on the law. After that, on days when Abe had no passengers, he rowed across the river to attend Pate's trials. He grew increasingly interested in court procedures and the law. He also borrowed a book of Indiana laws from an Indiana lawyer and educated himself, just as Pate had suggested.

During the time Abe worked along the Ohio River, merchants and store owners on the Indiana landings got a good look at the tall young man. The merchants noticed that he was a strong, diligent worker. James Gentry was the owner of one of the largest farms in the Pigeon Creek area and also operated a landing on the Ohio River. One day, Gentry made Abe

this particular afternoon, the water in the millstream was too low to power the mill. Abe hitched the old mare to the grinder, gave her a kick, and started the grinding process. Trying to speed things up, he urged the horse to go faster: He clucked at the horse, whipped it, and shouted at it to "git up, you old hussy; git up!" Suddenly, the horse reared up on its hind legs and kicked Abe in the head. He fell to the ground, unconscious and bleeding. According to Lincoln's autobiography, just before he got kicked, Abe had started to yell, "Git up . . ." one more time to the horse. The kick cut his holler short. He spent the night unconscious and awoke the next day. As he regained consciousness, Abe finished the sentence he had started before everything went black: ". . . you old hussy!"

an attractive offer. He asked Lincoln to help take a flatboat of cargo and produce down the Mississippi River to New Orleans. Abe eagerly accepted.

Abe and Gentry's son, Allen, pushed their flatboat off the Indiana landing in spring of 1829. It was a 1,200-mile voyage down the Ohio River and into the Mississippi River. The young men navigated the boat with long poles to avoid snags and sandbars. They maneuvered the boat among steamboats, ferries, and other river craft. Undoubtedly, Abe was excited to get his first glimpse at life away from the frontier. New Orleans was the first big city he had ever seen. As the harbor came into view, he looked around in amazement. The port was crowded with sailing ships from distant countries, and sailors and merchants from all over the world roamed the docks and streets of the city.

In New Orleans, young Abe got his first glimpse of African slavery. In those days, more than 200 slave dealers did business in New Orleans. Abe never forgot the horrible sight of African men, women, and children, draped in heavy chains, being driven along to be auctioned off like cattle.

The two young men sold their cargo and their flatboat in New Orleans and took a steamboat back to Indiana. For the three-month trip, Lincoln collected $24—a good sum of money at the time.

Early in 1830, Thomas Lincoln once again got the itch to move. He had heard magnificent stories about Illinois, a land where, instead of forests, lush prairies rolled on for endless miles. With their ox-drawn wagon crammed full of belongings, the Lincolns joined 11 other pioneers who wanted to trade their Indiana homes for a new start on the rich, black soil of Illinois.

On the Prairie

On March 1, 1830, the Lincolns and 11 other travelers left Indiana for Illinois. The two-week journey was slow and tedious. During the days, the frost-hardened trails started to thaw under the warm spring sun. The wagon wheels sank into the muck, making each mile seem twice as long. At night, the ground froze up again. In the mornings, streams were covered by a thin skin of ice. As the pioneers forded the streams, the hooves of their oxen punched holes in the frozen layer. Step by step, the ice broke away and disappeared into the trickling current.

The travelers brought along a dog that trotted beside the string of wagons. One day, the dog lagged far behind and did not catch up until the party had crossed a creek. Finally missing the mutt, the travelers looked back and saw him whining and

One of the most important jobs on a frontier farm in the 1800s was clearing forests. From the time Lincoln was very young, he was skillful with an ax and one of his chores was to split wood to make fence rails. Later, as a presidential candidate, he gained the nickname "the Railsplitter."

jumping on the opposite bank, afraid to cross. It hardly made sense to turn the oxen around and ford the stream again, just to save the dog. After a discussion, the majority decided that the party would have to leave the dog behind. Abe, however, could not bear the idea of abandoning the poor animal. Pulling off his shoes and socks, he waded across the creek and carried the dog back to the waiting wagons. According to Abe, the dog's excited affection was well worth braving the icy waters.

When the company reached Illinois, the Lincolns settled on 10 acres in Macon County, near Decatur. Once again, Tom Lincoln built a cabin for his family, this time with Abe's help. Still powerful with an ax, Abe chopped down trees and put together a split-rail fence that ran around the entire 10-acre plot. Noticing Abe's fine work, the Macon County sheriff, Major John Warnick, hired Abe and his cousin John Hanks to make a fence for him. With the money he earned, Abe bought his first set of new clothes. He had to split 400 rails for each yard of the brown fabric—dyed with white walnut bark—needed to stitch him a pair of trousers. When the job was finished, Abe had split 3,000 rails for the sheriff.

Abe stayed with his family during their first prairie winter. The winter of 1830–1831 was long remembered in Illinois as "the winter of the deep snow." That year, the snow seemed to fall, not by the flake, but by the shovelful. The snowy weather was accompanied by bitterly cold temperatures. Many livestock animals froze to death. On one afternoon, Abe's canoe tipped over as he crossed the Sangamon River, and his feet froze. He spent two weeks laid up as his feet healed from frostbite.

With his feet wrapped tightly in deerskin moccasins and confined to the house for two weeks, young Abe had plenty of time to think. He stared at the snow piled high outside the window and wondered what he should do when spring came. At age 21, he was getting restless to build a life of his own. He could buy a piece of land, as John Hanks had done, but he hated farm work. The previous summer, a visitor to Decatur had delivered a political address. Both Abe and his cousin John Hanks were in the crowd. When the speaker finished, Hanks declared that Abe could give a better speech. The speaker invited Abe to take his place on the platform. Abe stepped up and delivered an eloquent speech about the navigation of the Sangamon River. The visiting speaker was so impressed with the oration that he encouraged Abe to continue reading and speaking.

Perhaps, Abe thought, he should pursue a career as a lawyer. Before he had a chance to make up his mind, however, his cousin John Hanks showed up with an idea of his own. Hanks asked Abe to ride with him to Decatur to meet a businessman named Denton Offutt. The two cousins also invited Abe's step-brother, John Johnston, to come along.

The interview with Offutt turned out to be one of the most important events in Abe's early life. Offutt was considered the merchant prince of the Sangamon River. At a tavern in Decatur, he discussed with the three young men his plans for prosperity in the region. Offutt had traveled to Illinois from Lexington, Kentucky, and had brought with him a suitcase filled with moneymaking ideas. America's prairies could produce enormous crops. Still, other than by the rivers, there was no way to transport the crops to wide markets. Offutt's idea was to buy cargoes of grain and pork in Illinois and market them in New Orleans. For anyone who joined his business venture, he promised great rewards.

Hanks had met Offutt already and was hoping to persuade Lincoln and Johnston to trust the aspiring businessman. Hanks did not need to say a word. To Lincoln and Johnston, Offutt appeared to be a man of vision and enterprise. The three were drawn into Offutt's grand ideas, believing that there was no way they could fail.

Offutt told the young men that corn and pork would bring good prices at towns along the Sangamon River and in New Orleans. He wanted the three to handle his flatboat of cargo on its way down the river. Of course, Lincoln already had valuable experience in this type of work. Offutt offered

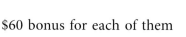

the men 50 cents per day and a $60 bonus for each of them when the job was done. They accepted the wages. They would leave in early spring.

NEW SALEM

In mid April of 1831, Lincoln, Hanks, and Johnston launched their flatboat on the Sangamon River. On April 19, early in the trip, the boat became lodged on the dam of the Rutledge Mill at New Salem, Illinois. Almost immediately, the boat began to tip and take on water. Lincoln and the others worked frantically to lighten the load in the boat's stern. Soon, the boat started to level out, but it still was heavy with water. Lincoln went ashore and borrowed an augur to bore a hole in the bow. As soon as he drilled the hole, the river water drained out, and he plugged up the opening. The men then lifted the boat and eased it over the dam. Impressed by Lincoln's ingenuity, Offutt swore that, after the trip to New Orleans, he would open a store in New Salem and hire Lincoln to be the manager.

In September 1831, after the New Orleans trip, 22-year-old Lincoln arrived in New Salem. He described himself as he was at the time as "a strange, friendless, uneducated, penniless boy." Undoubtedly, at six feet, four inches tall, rail thin, and with long, dangling arms that ended in oversized hands, he was quite an odd sight in the little town. He moseyed into town wearing a floppy-rimmed chip-straw hat slightly cocked on his strangely small head. Founded just two years earlier, New Salem stood on a bluff that overlooked the Sangamon River. The town was surrounded by woods. Only about 100 people called it their home. The residents lived in one- and two-room log cabins. At the time, New Salem was an unknown dot on the vast prairie. Settlers expected it to become a frontier boom town, however.

As promised, Offutt put Lincoln to work as his store's clerk, assisted by William "Slicky Bill" Greene. Without a spare penny between them for rent, Lincoln and Green slept on a single cot in the back of the store. Lincoln's gift for swapping stories and his simple honesty brought good business to Offutt's little store. Before long, Lincoln knew almost everyone in town and joined in community pastimes after store hours. He liked to run in foot-races, and, with his long legs, he demonstrated how he could outjump any other man in town. Several miles southwest of New Salem, there lived a group of bullies known as the Clary's Grove Boys. These wild and restless young men liked to challenge strangers to games of cards. Fairly or unfairly, the boys won the strangers' money and often beat them up, as well.

Inevitably, the Clary's Grove Boys heard about Offutt's clerk. Offutt did not help matters much by bragging about how Lincoln was not only the smartest man but also the strongest man. The Clary's Grove Boys had no interest in Lincoln's mind. They were eager to test his fighting ability, however. Jack Armstrong, their leader, challenged Lincoln to a fistfight. Tough and brawny, Armstrong had won dozens of fighting contests. Lincoln, who preferred wrestling over fistfighting, wanted to change the rules of the duel. "I never tussled and scuffled and will not," Lincoln said. Egged on by Offutt and others who already were placing bets on the match, Armstrong agreed to wrestle instead of fight.

The outcome of the contest became a legend in New Salem, although not necessarily an agreed-on one. According to some accounts, Lincoln easily took down Armstrong. Other onlookers, however, claimed that Armstrong brought down Lincoln, but with an illegal, disqualifying move. Armstrong's crew of bullies, angered by the defeat of their champion, tried to gang up on Lincoln. They backed down, however, when Lincoln vowed to beat every one of them—but only by fighting one at a time. No matter what actually happened, the event shaped Lincoln's future in New Salem and beyond. The test of his strength and courage earned him the respect and admiration not only of the townspeople, but also of the Clary's Grove Boys. Even Jack Armstrong soon became Lincoln's lifelong friend.

Abe Lincoln *(depicted above)* worked as a clerk at Denton Offutt's general store in New Salem for $15 a month. Like most stores in small towns during that time, Offutt's store was a local meeting place where customers would exchange humorous tales and talk politics with the friendly clerk. Lincoln joined the local debate club and was often called on to draw up legal documents for citizens that were unable to read and write.

Interestingly, the rough country boys of the area were not offended by Lincoln's refusal to smoke or drink. (Lincoln instead fed his peculiar desire to read.) Perhaps Lincoln's ability to tell jokes and stories made up for his social awkwardness.

In any case, there was no denying his amazing, Hercules-like strength. He could hurl a cannonball farther than any competitor, and one man claimed that Lincoln could lift a box of rocks weighing between 1,000 and 1,300 pounds.

Lincoln's friendships were not limited to just the rough-and-tumble fellows of New Salem. He appealed to the town's more intellectual crowd as well. Once a week, the New Salem Debating Society met at James Rutledge's tavern. One day, Lincoln decided to participate. At first, he was nervous. As he spoke, however, he surprised everyone with the logic of his argument. "He was already a fine speaker," one debater recalled. "All he lacked was culture."

Lincoln was somewhat ashamed of his meager education and sought to improve himself. A fellow debater who was also the local schoolmaster, Mentor Graham, offered to coach Lincoln on the finer points of English grammar. Because there was very little business at Offutt's store, Lincoln had plenty of time to study and read. In 1832, however, the store closed, and Lincoln had to find some other form of work.

At 23, Lincoln decided to run for the Illinois state legislature. Everyone in town liked him, and he was rapidly becoming a great public speaker. His friends encouraged him to run. They believed that such a bright young man could have a real future in politics. Confidently, Lincoln announced his candidacy and his political platform. He wanted local improvements, such as better roads and canals. He prepared an in-depth study of the Sangamon River and proposed that it be dredged and cleared so that steamboats could make port at New Salem. Such a plan could insure a magnificent future for the frontier town.

Before Lincoln could start his campaign, however, a war broke out in northern Illinois. In May of 1832, Chief Black Hawk led the Sac and Fox Indians from the Iowa territory into their former homelands in northern Illinois. In 1804, these American Indian groups had lost their land to the United States in a shady and crooked treaty. The American Indians planned to reclaim the land that was rightfully theirs. The American Indians' return sparked panic among white settlers. Illinois governor John Reynolds quickly dispatched the state militia to stop what he called an invasion. Lincoln enlisted in a militia company and joined the march with his friend, First Sergeant Jack Armstrong. The troops drilled and marched, but they never once spotted a hostile American Indian. Years later, Lincoln joked about his three-month stint in the militia. He said that the men had "a good many bloody battles with mosquitoes."

By the time Lincoln returned to New Salem at the end of July, just two weeks remained until the election. Lincoln plunged into his campaign, but it was too late to make up for the time he had lost. On election day, he finished eighth out of 13 candidates. Still, in his own area of New Salem, he received 227 votes out of 300 cast.

After his defeat, Lincoln decided to return to the trade of a frontier merchant. He went into business with William Berry and opened his own general store in New Salem. Neither partner seemed to have the knack for business, and before long, the store failed. Shortly after, Berry died, leaving Lincoln with a $1,100 debt. This was an enormous amount of money in those days, especially for someone who had never earned more than a few dollars a month. Lincoln jokingly called it "the national debt," but he promised to repay every cent. Although it took him 15 years, he kept his word.

To support himself, Lincoln worked at all sorts of odd jobs. Once again, he split fence rails. He also hired himself out as a farmhand and helped at the local gristmill. Then, on May 7, 1833, he was appointed postmaster of New Salem. There was little mail to deliver because most people picked up their letters at the post office. When people failed to pick up their mail, Lincoln delivered it free of charge. Although business at the post office was slow and most of the job's tasks menial, he was glad to earn the few dollars that the position paid. Then, in the fall of 1833, he was appointed deputy county surveyor.

In 1834, Lincoln ran for state legislature again, as a candidate of the Whig Party. Established that same year, the Whig Party was created in opposition to President Andrew Jackson, whom critics nicknamed "King Andrew." Jackson enraged many people with his policies and actions regarding the Bank of the United States, American Indians, and the Supreme Court. Many critics charged that he abused his presidential powers. The name Whig came directly from British politics; it was the name of the faction that opposed royal tyranny. Because Sangamon County was large, it held four seats in the state legislature. In this election, Lincoln finished second. That finish made him one of the four men elected to the Illinois House of Representatives from Sangamon County.

Penniless, Lincoln had to borrow money to get to Vandalia, the state capital. A friend loaned him $200 to cover his expenses. Lincoln climbed into a stagecoach to head for his first session as a representative. In those days, Illinois lawmakers received $3 per day for expenses, but only while the legislature was in session. Lincoln still needed to earn a living outside of his political career. A fellow representative, John Todd Stuart, was a promising young attorney. He encouraged Lincoln to study law, which, he pointed out, was the ideal profession for anyone with political ambitions.

The idea of the law was not a new one for Lincoln. For years, going back to the days when he sat in Squire Pate's Kentucky courtroom, he had toyed with the idea of becoming a lawyer. He also had served on several juries. At the same time, Lincoln worried that he would struggle because he had had such little formal education. In the 1830s, however, few lawyers actually attended law school. Instead, they "read law" in the office of a practicing attorney until they learned enough to pass their exams.

Lincoln decided to study law entirely on his own. He borrowed some law books from Stuart and bought some others at an auction. Day after day, he read and memorized legal codes and precedents. Back in New Salem, he recited aloud from

Once immensely popular and seen as the representative of the common man, Andrew Jackson's opponents accused him of abusing his presidential powers after his unprecedented veto of the bank bill. This cartoon depicts Jackson as King Andrew the First, a tyrannical king trampling on the Constitution.

one of his law books as he walked. On warm afternoons, he stretched out underneath a tree and read for hours. For nearly three years, Lincoln studied and read. Finally, on March 1, 1837, he passed his exams and became a lawyer.

By that time, the state legislature was moving from Vandalia to Springfield, which had been named the new capital of Illinois. In 1836, Lincoln had been elected to serve a second term in the legislature. A new apportionment had been made for this election, and Sangamon County's delegation—the largest in the state—consisted of nine men. Each of these men, including Lincoln, stood over six feet tall. They became known as the "Long Nine." Lincoln also had accepted a position as junior partner in John Todd Stuart's law office in Springfield. There was only one thing left to do: pack up his belongings and say good-bye to his friends in New Salem. A new life was waiting for him in Springfield.

Putting
Down Roots

On April 15, 1837, Abraham Lincoln trotted into Spring-field on a borrowed horse, with his belongings stuffed tightly into the saddlebags. His first stop was the general store of A.Y. Ellis & Company, on the courthouse square. There, he intended to purchase a single bed, complete with mattress, sheets, blankets, and a pillow. Joshua Speed, one of the store's proprietors, waited on Lincoln. As Speed showed him around the store, the two of them struck up a friendly conversation. Lincoln explained that he recently had been admitted to the bar and had traveled to Springfield to become John Todd Stuart's law partner. In time, Lincoln said, he hoped to build his own law office with an adjacent sleeping room.

Certainly, Speed already had heard a great deal about Lincoln. In 1836, Lincoln had taken part in a heated debate right there in Springfield. Wealthy Springfield resident George Forquer had left the Whig party to join the Democrats. As a reward, the Democratic Party appointed Forquer register of the land office. Forquer desperately wanted to crush Lincoln, a Whig, in a debate. Forquer made a so-called "slasher-gaff" speech in which he dealt mostly in ridicule and sarcasm. Standing nearby, Lincoln never interrupted. He politely awaited his turn to make a rebuttal. When Forquer was finished, Lincoln calmly walked to the podium and began to speak. Joshua Speed was among the crowd and said later that he never had heard a more effective speaker. "He carried the crowd with him," Speed recalled, "and swayed them as he pleased." As most of the town knew, Forquer recently had attached a new lightning rod to the roof of his house. Lincoln chose to use this well-known piece of information in his speech. According to *The Life of Abraham Lincoln*, he said, "I would rather die now, than, like [Forquer] change my politics, and simultaneously with the change, receive an office worth three thousand dollars per year, and then have to erect a lightning rod over my house, to protect a guilty conscience from an offended God." What Lincoln meant was that he would rather die true to his beliefs than be bought by the opposing side as Forquer had been. If Lincoln was unknown in the town before, the people of Springfield certainly heard about him after this famous debate. Speed had not met Lincoln until that sunny afternoon in April 1837, however.

After browsing through the store, Lincoln made his selections. Speed calculated the cost at $17. After considering the price, Lincoln said, "It is probably cheap enough, but I have not the money to pay. But if you will credit me until Christmas, and my experiment as a lawyer is a success, I will pay you then." He added, with a sigh, "If I fail in that, I will probably never be able to pay you at all." Speed thought about Lincoln's situation for a moment. Speed then told Lincoln that he had a large room above the store. He had plenty of extra space for a roommate if Lincoln was interested. Lincoln grabbed his saddlebags and carried them upstairs. After he came back down, he walked up to the counter and said, "Well, Speed, I'm moved."

At first glance, Speed and Lincoln seemed to be unlikely friends. At age 23, Speed was five years younger than Lincoln. Speed also was slim and handsome, with sparkling blue eyes and dark, curly hair. He had grown up in a wealthy family and attended the best private schools in Kentucky. He had studied for two years at St. Joseph's College. In contrast, Lincoln was lanky and awkward. Both his clothing and his appearance were unrefined. He had nothing to offer Speed except basic good manners, a desire to please, and sensitivity to the needs of others. At the same time, both men were ambitious—Speed for wealth and Lincoln for fame. Their friendship would last for years to come.

In the 1830s, Springfield, Illinois, was a typical frontier town. Although there were a few brick buildings, many of the residents still lived in log houses. The roads were wide, but they also were unpaved. There were no sidewalks, and hogs roamed freely through the dusty streets. It was the most cosmopolitan and sophisticated town in which Lincoln had ever lived, however.

Founded in 1821, Springfield had grown into a thriving community of 1,500 residents by the time Lincoln arrived. The Sangamon County Courthouse stood in the center of town. The streets that ran north and south were numbered; those that ran east and west were named after American presidents. The courthouse, soon to be replaced by the new state capitol, was surrounded by 19 dry goods stores, 7 groceries, 4 drugstores, 2 clothing stores, and a bookstore. Visitors had four hotels from which to choose. In addition to a number of schools and a high school academy, the town boasted six churches. Eighteen doctors and 11 lawyers had opened practices there. This booming pioneer city was where Lincoln put down his roots. For the rest of his life, he considered this place his hometown.

In 1836, while serving as a representative to the Illinois legislature, Lincoln became a licensed attorney and moved to Springfield, Illinois. One of his major achievements was the transfer of the state capital from Vandalia to Springfield in 1837. On the right corner is the Stuart & Lincoln law firm.

Lincoln found easy acceptance in Springfield, mostly because he arrived as Stuart's partner. Stuart was one of the most prominent and successful lawyers in town. Unlike most beginning lawyers, who had to hunt for business, Lincoln started out with a full practice. Stuart was concentrating on winning a seat in the U.S. House of Representatives, and he handed over many of his cases to Lincoln.

The Stuart & Lincoln law office occupied a single room on the second floor of a building in a line of brick buildings on Fifth Street known as Hoffman's Row. The row was just a block north of the courthouse square. Here, in a scantily furnished room that housed a library consisting of a couple of volumes of *Illinois Reports*, Stuart and Lincoln received clients, heard their complaints, and decided what—if any—action should be taken. Lincoln had no difficulty performing the routine work of the office, such as drafting wills or writing deeds. He had done tasks such as these for his neighbors in New Salem even before he passed the bar exam.

Most of the firm's cases involved appearances before justices of the peace, few of whom were lawyers. With these procedures, too, Lincoln was well acquainted, as he often had attended the Bowling Green court in New Salem. The more complex cases went to trial before a circuit court. There, again, Lincoln had had some prior experience, both as an observer and as a witness. Now, as a licensed attorney, he had a much more pressing responsibility: to fully master the forms and procedures of litigation. Even a minor, technical error could lose a case for a client.

From the beginning of the partnership, Stuart & Lincoln carried a heavy load of cases. As early as the July 1837 term of the Sangamon County Circuit Court, the firm had 19 common-law cases and 7 chancery cases on the docket—more than twice as many cases as the firm's rival, Logan & Baker. Common-law cases followed a highly formal set of proceedings and precedents, while chancery cases followed somewhat more flexible rules. Lincoln always had as much business as he could handle. His practice was not confined to Sangamon County. The circuit court met in Springfield only twice a year, each time for a two-week session. No lawyer could earn his living in a single county. Like most lawyers, Lincoln traveled on the broad, nine-county circuit in central and eastern Illinois that the judges made. The judges traveled from one county to another and held sessions that lasted from two days to a week. From time to time, Lincoln appeared at court in Bloomington, in McLean County, as well as in the counties of Tazewell, Macon, Morgan, and others in central Illinois.

Although Lincoln had a full schedule, money was still tight. With so many lawyers practicing in Springfield, Stuart & Lincoln had to keep their rates competitive. For most cases, Lincoln charged a fee of $5. Other cases ranged in price from $2.50 to $10.

LOVE IS ETERNAL

Lincoln's efforts to achieve poise in his public life mirrored his internal struggle to bring stability and confidence to his personal life, which still was unshaped and shaky. He was unsure of who he was or how he desired to be seen by others. He liked to associate with the aristocrats of Springfield, yet he also wanted to be "one of the boys." His inner uncertainty affected his relationships with women, as well.

Back in New Salem, Lincoln had fallen in love for the first time in his life. Historians debate, however, whether this relationship actually took place. According to legend, Lincoln had a love affair with Ann Rutledge, the daughter of a local tavern owner. The relationship came to a tragic end when Ann died suddenly, at age 22, of typhoid fever. About a year after Ann Rutledge's death, Lincoln pursued a halfhearted courtship with Mary Owen, which came to nothing. Awkward and nervous, Lincoln considered giving up on women altogether. Then, one night, at a party given by a wealthy acquaintance, Lincoln met Mary Todd.

The daughter of Robert S. Todd, a prosperous merchant and banker in Lexington, Kentucky, Mary grew up in luxury. She was attended by slaves and educated in private schools. Unable to get along with her stepmother, she decided to visit her sister Elizabeth Edwards in Springfield in 1839. Mary Todd was not quite 21 years old when she arrived in Springfield. Immediately, she captured the attention of the local men with her smooth, fair complexion, her chestnut hair, and her strikingly vivid blue eyes.

As soon as he met her, Lincoln told Mary Todd that he wanted to dance with her "in the worst way." As Mary later recalled with a laugh, he did just that. He was quite clumsy on his oversized feet. Lincoln was enchanted by Mary Todd's intelligence and spunk. He began to see her regularly, at parties, on walks, and on horseback rides. Mary Todd was different from any woman Lincoln had ever known. Around her, he could

After a long courtship, Lincoln married Mary Todd (1818–1882) on November 4, 1842. The daughter of a banker, Mary grew up in comfort, attending fine schools, learning dance, drama, French, and music. Although Abe was often absent from home practicing law and campaigning for political office, she shared her husband's ambition. As a staunch supporter of the Union cause, she defended Lincoln during the growing crisis caused by slavery.

relax, mostly because she led the conversation. He simply sat back and listened, charmed by her wit and culture. Although Lincoln lacked social graces and a handsome face, his honesty, courtesy, and kindness won Mary Todd's affections. Before long, the two began to talk about marriage.

As soon as Lincoln made a commitment to marry Mary Todd, he began to have second thoughts. Even though he was 30 years old, he worried that he would be unable to support a wife. His income from his legal practice was now more than $1,000 a year, and he also had his small salary as a state legislator. Still, neither job held a guaranteed future. His law partnership was about to dissolve. Stuart had been elected to the U.S. House of Representatives. He spent much of his time in political business and contributed little to the law practice. Because his reelection to a second term seemed almost certain, there was no reason for him to continue his empty partnership with Lincoln.

As for Lincoln's own political career, he was not even assured an income from the state legislature, especially because the state of Illinois was suffering from debt and bankruptcy. Some of the state's financial problems had come about because of the Sangamon County Long Nine's influence in the legislature. The Long Nine, including Lincoln, had voted for some ambitious improvements to the state's transportation systems, such as new roads and canals, when there was no money to pay for the upgrades. As a result, Lincoln's popularity as a legislator was on the decline.

In the 1840 election, Lincoln was no longer the candidate with the most votes. Many voters in rural precincts rejected him. He already had decided not to run for reelection when his present term was up. Lincoln was a man with an uncertain income who had no savings and did not own a house. He probably still owed something on his "national debt" from his New Salem days. There was no way he could offer Mary Todd the life of luxury to which she was accustomed.

Money was not the only factor that made Lincoln feel anxious about marriage, however. He was afraid that he would not be a worthy husband. He wondered, too, whether he truly loved Mary Todd enough to marry her. Finally, his nerves got the better or him. In early January 1841, he resolved to break the engagement. He wrote Mary Todd a letter in which he told her that he did not love her. Joshua Speed tried to persuade Lincoln to burn the letter. He encouraged Lincoln to talk to Mary in person, instead. "Words are forgotten," said Speed. "But once you put your words in writing . . . they stand as a living and eternal monument against you." Reluctantly, Lincoln heeded his friend's advice. He went to the Edwards's mansion. When he told Mary that he no longer loved her, she burst into tears. Deeply moved by her pain, Lincoln pulled her close and kissed her. Then he walked out the door, believing that it was over between them.

For several days, Mary Todd brooded over Lincoln, trying to understand the reason for his change of heart. Finally, she decided that it was because he was in love with another woman. She wrote him a letter to let him know that she accepted the breakup. At the same time, she told him that she had not changed her mind about him; she felt the same as always.

Instead of feeling relieved, Lincoln was devastated by Mary Todd's letter. It made him realize what he had lost. Perhaps, he thought, he really did love her. In the weeks that followed, he fell into a deep depression. Although he was able to perform his daily tasks at first, the burden of guilt and sadness eventually crept into every aspect of his life. He took to his bed for almost a week, unwilling to speak to anyone except Speed and his doctor. His collapse became the subject of local gossip. Some people thought that he was pretending to be ill. Others whispered that he was about to die. Still others claimed that he was grieving because Mary Todd had broken their engagement.

By the end of January, Lincoln was able to push his way through his daily routine again, but his mood was listless and broody. He tried to bring his life back under control. He dropped out of the Edwards's social circle and tried to bury his cares in his law practice. In April, he entered into a new law partnership with Stephen T. Logan. The office of Logan &

Lincoln was on the east side of North Fifth Street in Springfield. The practice served many clients, but Lincoln received only one-third of the fees instead of his usual half. Despite the drop in pay, he at least had a reliable income. He was still far from happy, however.

In the summer of 1841, Lincoln's good friend Joshua Speed, who had moved back to Kentucky, got married. In a letter to Lincoln, Speed bragged about how wonderful his marriage was. All at once, Lincoln's fears and anxieties about marriage lifted. If Speed was happy in marriage, he could be, too. Lincoln began to see Mary again, but just as friends. The two had to meet in secret, however. After Lincoln broke the engagement, the Edwards clan rejected him. They bluntly told Mary that she should never marry Lincoln: Their personalities, education, and upbringing were so different that they never would live happily ever after as husband and wife. During their private meetings, however, the couple rediscovered that they had much in common, and they grew closer than they had been before. Then, their relationship got just the boost it needed when they joined forces in a political scuffle.

In February 1842, the State Bank of Illinois, which Lincoln often had defended in the state legislature, was forced to close. The banknotes issued by the bank became worthless. State auditor James Shields declared that the bank's notes would not be accepted to pay taxes. Immediately, the Whigs took advantage of the crisis. They attacked the Democratic administration of the state—especially Shields.

Lincoln, a Whig, began to write short articles to a local newspaper, the *Sangamo Journal*, under the pseudonym of "Rebecca." The fictional Rebecca was a rough countrywoman, uneducated but shrewd. Lincoln's letters from the "Lost Townships" attacked Democratic policies and poked fun at Shields. In the letters, Lincoln allowed his sense of humor to run free. He ridiculed Shields at every opportunity. He let Mary Todd and one of her friends help sharpen the barbs in one letter before it appeared in the *Sangamo Journal* on September 2. Carried away by the excitement, the two young women decided to write their own letter. That rather clumsy letter pushed things a little too far. It struck the state auditor at his most vulnerable point—his vanity.

Although Shields was a man of excellent character, he was somewhat pompous. He also believed that he was irresistible to women. The letter written by the two young women took cheap shots at his exaggerated opinion of himself. Hot-tempered and excitable, Shields had no sense of humor. After the publication of Mary Todd's letter, he demanded that the paper reveal the name of his anonymous assailant. To protect the women, Lincoln took responsibility for all of the "Lost Townships" letters. Shields demanded that Lincoln write a full and absolute retraction of all the offensive references to Shields that he had made in the letters. Lincoln refused to apologize. To save his character, Shields challenged Lincoln to a duel.

Because dueling was outlawed in Illinois, Shields and Lincoln agreed to meet at a place in Missouri, across the Mississippi River from the town of Alton. As the man being challenged, Lincoln had the right to name the weapons to be used. He chose broadswords. During the Black Hawk War, Lincoln had gained some experience with cavalry swords. With his height and long arms, broadswords would give Lincoln an advantage over Shields, who was only five feet, nine inches tall.

Lincoln later said that he had no intentions of hurting Shields, except in self-defense. As it turned out, however, the duel was called off at the last minute. Lincoln assured Shields that the "Lost Townships" letters were not meant to damage his personal character but were written only for political effect. With that, the two men shook hands and returned to Illinois. Ashamed by the whole ordeal, Lincoln and Mary agreed never to speak of the incident again.

One good thing came out of the mess: a new engagement to Mary Todd. She was so touched by Lincoln's chivalry in protecting her contributions to the "Lost Townships" letters that she

JAMES SHIELDS.

General James Shields (1810–1879) was the only person in U.S. history to serve as a senator for three different states—Illinois, Minnesota, and Missouri. When he was Illinois state auditor, he nearly fought a duel with Lincoln over inflammatory letters he thought Lincoln had written to the *Sangamon Journal*. Just before engaging in combat, Lincoln and Shields called off the duel after Lincoln apologized.

once again accepted his proposal. On Friday evening, November 4, 1842, the couple was married at the Edwards's mansion. As storm clouds rumbled outside, Lincoln slipped a wedding ring on his new bride's finger. He had ordered three words to be engraved on the inside of the ring: "Love is eternal."

After the ceremony, the newlyweds climbed into a carriage and rode off in the rain to their first home—a room at the Globe Tavern boardinghouse. For $4 a week, the Lincolns rented an 8-foot-by-14-foot room on the second floor and ate their meals in a shared dining room. Although the Globe Tavern was a typical lodging for a young married couple, it lacked the luxuries to which Mary Todd Lincoln was accustomed. Undoubtedly, Mary was a bit uncomfortable in her new home, but she never complained to anyone.

On August 1, 1843, Mary gave birth to their first child at the Globe Tavern—a son named Robert Todd Lincoln. With a newborn baby, the Lincolns realized that they needed more room. In the fall, they moved to a three-bedroom cottage at 214 South Fourth Street. They paid $100 per year in rent. Early in 1844, Lincoln purchased a permanent home at the corner of Eighth and Jackson streets. On the ground floor of the cozy house were three rooms—a parlor, a kitchen, and a sitting room with a fireplace. In the half loft above, there were two bedrooms heated with wood-burning stoves. The ceilings upstairs were so steeply slanted that Lincoln had only four feet of space in which he could stand up straight.

During these years, Lincoln continued his day-to-day activities at the law office. In his early years, Lincoln had looked on his legal career simply as fuel for his real aspirations in politics. Now that he had a family, however, he focused his energies on earning a living as a prominent prairie lawyer.

5

Diligent Abe

"The leading rule for the lawyer, as for the man, of any calling [occupation], is diligence," said Lincoln. Lincoln practiced what he preached. He worked hard and handled every type of business that possibly could land on the desk of a prairie lawyer. He earned some money by filing the many bankruptcy claims caused by the economic depression of the 1840s. Most of his work came from the drafting of wills, petitions, and petty suits, however. Business was so good that Lincoln and Logan traded their cramped office on Fifth Street for one in the newly constructed Tinsley Building, the premier location for any thriving business.

Lincoln learned much from his partner. Logan was nine years older than Lincoln and a prominent lawyer in Sangamon County. Logan's sharp analytical mind and his knowledge of legal proceedings made him an intimidating opponent in the courtroom. With his harsh, scratchy voice, however, he was an ineffective public speaker. Juries were put off by his rumpled hair, his battered figure, and skin that was said to resemble a raisin. Logan was aware of these shortcomings and hoped that Lincoln could win the admiration of the juries. During Lincoln's years as surveyor and a state legislator, he made a wide array of acquaintances. Almost everyone in Sangamon County recognized his lanky figure. Thanks to a remarkable memory, he could recall the name, hometown, and family of nearly every person called to jury duty. In the courtroom, Lincoln created an easy atmosphere, as though he were having a personal conversation with the jury. He always kept things simple. He rarely used technical language or introduced intricate concepts. Often, he used a homespun anecdote to illustrate a point.

In one murder case, a physician claimed that the accused man was insane. The doctor had studied the criminal's physical behavior and pointed out that he constantly picked at his head. Lincoln was not convinced by this diagnosis. "Now," Lincoln remarked, "I sometimes pick my head, and those joking fellows at Springfield tell me that there may be a living, moving cause for it [lice], and that the trouble isn't at all on the inside. It's only a case for fine-tooth combs."

To Logan's surprise, Lincoln proved to be much more than an able courtroom litigator. His in-depth studies of cases helped him to become a well-rounded master of law. Up to this point, Lincoln had had only a minimal grasp of the law. Under Logan's tutelage, he grew quite ambitious with his legal work. In 1841, the Illinois Supreme Court moved into the statehouse at Springfield, bringing with it an extensive collection of legal reports and reference texts. Lincoln spent many nights in the Supreme Court library, searching out precedents that applied to his cases. With his superior knowledge, he made multiple appearances before the Illinois Supreme Court.

In the fall of 1844, Logan talked about ending his partnership with Lincoln. He planned to go into business with his son.

This time, Lincoln was unshaken by the news. His political aspirations still simmered in the back of his mind. He wanted to run for Congress. Knowing that Logan planned to do the same, he feared that their ambitions might clash and cause damage to the partnership. Lincoln considered opening up his own law practice. He already had a partner in mind, a young beginner named William H. Herndon.

One crisp fall morning, Lincoln came dashing up the stairs of the Tinsley Building. On the third floor, he found Herndon, intently studying his law papers. "Billy," Lincoln interrupted, "do you want to enter into a partnership with me in the law business?" Flustered by the question, Herndon wondered why Lincoln would choose him—someone so inexperienced. Lincoln stated, simply, that he trusted Billy, and if Billy could trust him, it could be a good partnership. Herndon quickly accepted the offer.

Herndon was not the only person confused by Lincoln's choice. Many people found the new partnership puzzling. As an established, prominent lawyer, Lincoln could have picked any number of distinguished Illinois attorneys. Lincoln had been watching William Herndon, however, and he believed that the studious young man had a promising future as a lawyer. Political reasons also swayed Lincoln's decision. By 1844, the Whig Party had split into two camps. The leadership of the first camp came from the older Whigs, men such as the respectable Stuarts and Edwardses. Although few in number, these men were rich and staunch in family tradition. Now, however, the majority of Whig voters were self-made men, men with power who scorned the older leadership and wanted a hand in shaping policy. If Lincoln were to run for Congress, he would need the support of both factions to win. His marriage to Mary Todd handed him approval from the old leadership. He still needed to woo the shrewd, self-made, new boys in town, however. Lincoln knew that Herndon was a leader in this group. A professional alliance

William Herndon (1818–1891) became Lincoln's law partner in 1841. After the dissolution of the Whig Party, both men became members of the Republican Party. Firmly opposed to slavery, Herndon claimed that he helped change Lincoln's views. Herndon believed that the only way to end slavery was through mass uprising and felt that Lincoln moved too slowly on the issue once he became president.

with Billy Herndon would give Lincoln an edge in gaining the support of the younger Whigs.

Herndon was nine years Lincoln's junior. Lincoln always called Herndon "Billy," while Herndon called his partner "Mr. Lincoln." They were about as opposite as two men could get. Lincoln was tall, slow-moving, and careless in his appearance. Herndon was short, quick, and a dandy dresser, decked out in patent-leather shoes and kid gloves. In disposition, Lincoln was melancholy, with occasional bursts of bizarre humor. Herndon was upbeat, optimistic, and bubbled with ideas and enthusiasm. When Lincoln dealt with the law, he disliked generalities and cautiously moved in logical progression from one fact to the next. In contrast, Herndon jumped ahead, using intuition to formulate his conclusions.

At the office in the Tinsley Building, Lincoln & Herndon gladly accepted whatever clients came along. They handled cases of murder, burglary, assault, embezzlement, and just about every other kind of crime. Sometimes, their clients were innocent. At other times, they were guilty. Lincoln believed that every client, whether innocent or guilty, was entitled to legal representation. Bravely, Lincoln also handled delicate social cases, such as those that involved slavery. In those days, opinions about the institution of slavery often led to violent debates. As early as 1841, Lincoln appeared before the Illinois Supreme Court in the case of *Bailey v. Cromwell*. He represented Nance, an African-American woman whom someone had tried to sell as a slave. Illinois was a free state: Within its borders, slavery was illegal. Lincoln argued, as quoted in David Herbert Donald's *Lincoln*, "The presumption of law was, in this state, that every person was free without regard to color . . . the sale of a free person is illegal." The courts agreed.

Lincoln did not necessarily argue for emancipation, however. In 1847, he represented Robert Matson, a man who was trying to recover a runaway slave. Matson was a Kentucky farmer who had brought his slaves with him across the Ohio

River into the free state of Illinois. He planned to stay only for a while, to work his farmland in southern Illinois and then go back to Kentucky. While he was in Illinois, however, one of his slaves escaped. The abolitionists in the area filed a suit against Matson on the grounds that, as far back as the late eighteenth century, the Northwest Ordinance had forbidden the introduction of slavery into the territory of Illinois.

In court, Lincoln admitted the abolitionists' point: The slaves would be free if Matson had brought them to Illinois to live. Matson, however, had no intention of settling permanently in Illinois. He therefore had the right of transit, which allowed slaveholders to pass through a free state or territory with their slaves. Luckily for the escaped slave, this time, the circuit court ruled against Lincoln. Matson left for Kentucky immediately, without paying his attorney's fees. For Lincoln, this case was just business. It did not reflect his personal views on slavery. He believed that slavery was both immoral and poor economic policy. He had voiced this opinion when he was a state legislator.

Arguing cases of all sorts, Lincoln and Herndon traveled the wide circle of circuit courts. It took at least 10 weeks to complete the circuit. Usually, Lincoln rode his rickety horse, Old Tom. He carried a change of clothes and the necessary legal papers in his saddlebags. In those days, roads were few, and the roads that did exist offered a crude, bumpy ride. Many streams had no bridges on which to cross. When Lincoln and Herndon came to a stream, Lincoln—who had the longest legs—waded in to explore the depth. If Lincoln could get across, Herndon followed. At night, they stopped wherever they could find lodgings. Sometimes, they crowded into a room with 20 other circuit-riding lawyers.

Meanwhile, Lincoln's long business trips caused tension at home. In 1846, Mary had given birth to a second son, Edward. While her husband was away on the circuit, Mary had to take care of all the household chores and care for the children. Hot-tempered and bold, she was not afraid to tell her husband how she felt. Sometimes she flew into terrible rages. For the most part, however, Abe and Mary were loyal and supportive to each other. Their politics also helped to keep them together.

RIDING THE CIRCUIT

Although Abraham Lincoln had less than two years of formal education, he loved learning and continued to seek out information to increase his knowledge on various subjects. In his early adult years, he read law books and would draw up legal papers for the citizens of New Salem, Illinois. In 1836, Lincoln became a licensed attorney and a junior partner of John T. Stuart's Springfield, Illinois, law office, and later had his own practice with William H. Herndon. Although he began his legal career benefiting from the experienced Stuart's caseload, Lincoln still had a very limited education and no established ties, so he had to scramble for his own clients. Within the first decade of his career, he quickly ascended to the top tier of his profession and clients sought out his services. He earned a good income for that time, about $1,200 to $1,500 a year, and his caseloads became more substantial. He went from handling small-time lawsuits like dealing with crop damage caused by wandering livestock, ownership of hogs and horses, small debts, libel, and assault and battery to attracting corporate clients and even a lucrative retainer with the Illinois Central Railroad.

Since Springfield courts were in session for part of the year, frontier lawyers and judges would ride the circuit, holding court at rural county seats. Twice a year for over 20

Like her husband, Mary was an ardent Whig. Her encouragement was crucial for the next phase in Lincoln's career: a run for the U.S. Congress.

years, Lincoln covered 15 counties and about 8,000 square miles as an attorney in the Eighth Judicial Circuit, the largest in the state of Illinois. Ten percent of his state practice also brought him before the Illinois Supreme Court. He gained notoriety and fame as an attorney due to his storytelling abilities and debating skills, and since he still held political ambitions he used his popularity on the circuit to meet new people and advance his political career.

Practicing both law and politics simultaneously was natural to Lincoln. As a member of the Illinois state legislature, politics remained his principal interest, but he needed to continue working at his law practice in order to support his growing family and his political activities. One favorable aspect of combining law with politics was the broad exposure to the important issues of the time, issues that he would have to handle when he became president: taxation, corporate behavior, and slavery.

When Lincoln finally suspended his practice at the age of 51 in the middle of his campaign for the presidency, he was well respected and widely known throughout the American West. He had achieved material success, self-confidence, political connections, and professional stature. Had he opted to stay in the legal profession rather than seek the presidency, historians suggest that Lincoln would have become one of the most influential attorneys in America.

IN WASHINGTON

Lincoln had lost the Whig nomination for Congress in 1843, but he was eager to try again in the 1846 election. In the fall of 1845, a full year before the election, he began actively to work to secure the Whig nomination. His primary opponent was John Hardin of Jacksonville, Illinois, a man who already had served two terms in Congress.

Throughout the campaign, the two opponents tried to outmaneuver each other. Hardin's friends suggested nominating Lincoln for governor, knowing that it would throw him off the track of Congress. When Lincoln's supporters got word of this plan, they proposed Hardin for governor. Neither man ran for the post. As he surveyed the congressional district, Lincoln knew that he had support from Sangamon and Menard counties, but he expected Morgan and Scott counties to vote for Hardin. It was critical, therefore, for him to win the northern part of the district, especially Tazewell County. For help, Lincoln went to Benjamin James, the editor of the *Tazewell Whig* and a strong Lincoln supporter.

Lincoln's tactics worked. In late 1845, as he traveled the circuit, he secured endorsements from leading men throughout the district before anyone knew that Hardin wanted to serve another term. By January 1846, Lincoln had the nomination locked up. His democratic opponent was Peter Cartwright, a celebrated Methodist circuit-riding preacher who was famous for his devotion to Andrew Jackson-like principles. Although he was personally popular, Cartwright proved to be a poor political campaigner. On August 3, 1846, the voters of the Seventh District made their choice. They elected Abraham Lincoln to the U.S. House of Representatives by a greater margin than ever before.

Surprisingly, Lincoln was not as pleased with his victory as he had hoped to be. He was the only Whig representative from Illinois, and his party would have little influence on the Democratic administration of President James K. Polk. Because Lincoln had promised his constituents that he would serve only one term, he viewed his two years in Congress as an opportunity to help the Whig party find fresh leadership and adopt policies relevant to the times. He also devoted himself to promoting General Zachary Taylor for president in 1848.

On December 2, 1847, just a few days before the Thirteenth Congress convened, the Lincolns arrived in Washington. They moved into the boardinghouse of Mrs. Ann Sprigg. The house was located east of the Capitol, where the Library of Congress now stands. Eight other congressmen—all Whigs—boarded at the same house. Not long after the Lincolns' arrival, Mary became unhappy with the situation. Because few congressmen brought their wives with them to Washington, she lacked female companionship. Busy with his work, her husband was rarely at home. Mary appeared downstairs in the common room of the house only at mealtimes. The rest of the time she spent shut in a single room with the two boys. Immediately, she got the impression that the other congressmen in the house did not like her. Perhaps the noisy children bothered them. In the spring, Mary took the children and moved back to her father's house in Kentucky. The couple would have to live apart while Lincoln served his duties as a congressman.

At first, Lincoln hardly missed his wife. He was wrapped up in his congressional work. Because of his previous experience as a postmaster, he was assigned to the Committee of Post Offices and Post Roads. He also served on the Committee of Expenditures in the War Department. In Washington, Lincoln found the Whig Party in disarray. Although, overall, the Whigs had done well in the elections of 1846, the party leaders were doubtful that a Whig candidate would stand a chance in the upcoming presidential election of 1848. The Democratic administration of James Polk had been incredibly successful. President Polk had settled a long-simmering boundary dispute with Great Britain about the Oregon Territory. By signing into law the Walker Tariff, which imposed extremely low duties on imported goods, President Polk also set economic policy for the next decade. To top it all off, Polk presided over a successful war against Mexico that was about to add California and New Mexico to the Union. The odds of a Whig candidate beating the designated Democratic successor—Senator Lewis Cass—were slim to none.

The only issue on which the Democrats were vulnerable was Polk's role in bringing about the Mexican War. In 1847, in his annual address to Congress, Polk asked for additional funds to bring the war to a close. In a final triumphant note, he proclaimed that Mexico had started the war by invading the state of Texas, thereby striking the first blow and shedding the blood of American citizens on U.S. soil. The statement sparked a Whig attack on the Polk administration and Lincoln led the assault. On December 22, 1847, Lincoln presented to Congress a series of resolutions that required the president to provide the House with a detailing of all the events that led up to the war. Lincoln asserted that Polk must prove that the particular spot on which American blood was spilled actually belonged to the United States. With this challenge, Lincoln suggested that the American army had started the war by launching an unprovoked attack on a Mexican settlement.

Much to Lincoln's disappointment, no one in Washington paid much attention to his resolutions. In fact, his attack backfired, and years later, some of his comments came back to haunt him. Lincoln claimed, for instance, that Polk had acted unconstitutionally when he ordered American troops into war. Declaring war, Lincoln asserted, was the job of Congress, not the chief executive. This same argument later was used by Lincoln's enemies during the Civil War. At one point, Lincoln also made a statement about the right to revolution. He said, "Any people anywhere . . . have the right to rise up, and shake off the existing government, and form a new one that suits them better." No doubt, he had to eat these words when 11 Southern states seceded from the Union and formed their own government in 1860–1861.

Lincoln succeeded in at least one of his goals while in Congress: getting Zachary Taylor elected president in 1848. Lincoln managed an effective campaign, and he came away with the big prize that the Whigs had been hoping for. Immediately after the election, Lincoln did not seek any office as a reward for his help in the campaign. The highest office to be given to an Illinois Whig would be that of commissioner of the General Land Office. This position paid a hefty $3,000 salary and carried a great deal of power. Some of Lincoln's friends encouraged him to apply for the position. He hesitated at first but finally agreed. Because Lincoln's attacks on Polk had generated much public disapproval, however, President Taylor chose someone else. Staying true to his word, Lincoln did not run for a second term in Congress. Somewhat deflated, he had nothing else to do but return to Illinois to pick up his law practice where he had left off.

HONEST ABE

From 1849 to 1854, Lincoln practiced law more fervently than ever before. Finished with his service in Washington, he resettled his family into their little house on Eighth and Jackson streets in Springfield. His law practice now was his only source of income. For the time being, he tried to put his political career out of his mind. Illinois offered no future for an ambitious Whig politician. Once again, Lincoln and Herndon, working as a team, reestablished their prosperous law firm.

Lincoln's most famous murder case was one in which he defended William "Duff" Armstrong. Duff's parents had invited Lincoln to stay with them when he first moved to New Salem. As a way of thanking them, Lincoln took the case without charging a fee. Armstrong and a friend, James Norris, were jointly accused of killing a man named James Metzker during a drunken brawl near Havana, in Macon County, Illinois, on August 29, 1857. In court, it was proved that Norris hit the victim with an ox–yoke. Norris was sentenced to eight years in

Mary and Abe Lincoln raised their family in this house in Springfield for 17 years, until Abe was elected president. Instead of selling their home, the Lincolns decided to rent it out and store their furniture until their return. Unfortunately, Abe was assassinated and Mary could not bear returning to their home. Today the Lincoln home is a national historic site and is open to the public for guided tours.

the penitentiary for his crime. When Lincoln took Armstrong's case, it had not yet been determined whether Armstrong was responsible for a second injury to Metzker's body.

On May 7, 1858, the case was tried in Beardstown, Illinois. The prosecution's argument hinged on the testimony of star witness Charles Allen. Allen claimed to have seen every detail of the murder, at nine thirty at night, in the bright light of a full moon. After stressing to the jury the importance of Allen's statement, Lincoln pulled out a copy of the *Farmer's Almanac*.

He flipped to a page that showed that on August 29, 1857—the day of the assault—the moon was barely past its first quarter. On such a night, the light of the moon could not have been as bright as the witness had claimed. The information in the almanac discredited Allen's testimony.

As the jury left the courtroom to consider their verdict, Lincoln placed a hand on Hannah Armstrong's shoulder. As quoted in *Lincoln and His America, 1809–1865,* he gently assured her, "Aunt Hannah, your son will be free before sundown." The jury returned with a verdict of "not guilty."

During this time, Lincoln acquired a couple of nicknames. Many of his colleagues called him "Old Abe" because of his rugged appearance. Years of hard work had dug deep creases in his face, making him look much older than his 41 years. Around the circuit, however, most folks knew him as "Honest Abe." He was the lawyer who never lied. He showed fairness to his opponents, politeness in the courtroom, and utmost respect for the judges' rulings and decisions. In some notes that he wrote for a lecture to young law students in 1850, Lincoln referred to the common joke that all lawyers are dishonest. Here is what he said:

> Let no young man, choosing the law for a calling, for a moment yield to this popular belief. Resolve to be honest at all events; and if, in your own judgment, you cannot be an honest lawyer, resolve to be honest without being a lawyer. Choose some other occupation.

Just as Lincoln was reestablishing himself as a lawyer, tragedy struck the Lincoln household. Four-year-old Edward, who was often sick, suddenly became seriously ill with pulmonary tuberculosis. There was no cure for this deadly disease. After 52 days of suffering, he died, on February 1, 1850. Both parents were devastated, but to Mary Lincoln, it was an especially cruel blow. Eddie's death came shortly after the deaths of her father and her beloved grandfather. The loss of her son was almost too much for Mary to bear. She was exhausted from nursing the sick child day and night. Both Mary and Abraham Lincoln rejected the belief of some Christians that their son's death was part of some divine plan. The thought of an afterlife brought Mary little comfort.

A few weeks after Eddie's death, Mary found out that she was expecting another child. Ten months after Eddie passed away, William Wallace was born. Willie was named after Dr. William Wallace, who had married one of Mary's sisters. On April 4, 1853, she gave birth to another son, whom the Lincolns named Thomas. The boy was named for Abraham Lincoln's father, who recently had passed away. Thomas was born with an unusually large head. Playfully, Lincoln said that his newborn son looked like a little tadpole. The family gave the baby the nickname "Tad," which stuck with him for the rest of his life.

While Lincoln occupied himself with his law practice, the nation simmered with turmoil. The issue of slavery had opened a huge chasm of disagreements between the states of the North and the states of the South. For 30 years, the tension had swelled and ebbed. By 1850, however, the situation was nearing a break-ing point. A time was coming when someone would have to win, and someone would have to lose.

A Nation Divided

Long before the Civil War broke out, Northerners and Southerners rammed heads. From the time of the nation's founding, people throughout the United States held opposing views on slavery. The topic became especially heated in the early 1800s. Southern slaveholding states had much smaller white populations than Northern free states. Under the Constitution, the number of congressmen that each state could send to the House of Representatives was based on the total white population of the state. By 1820, rapid growth in the North had left the South with fewer than 45 percent of the seats in the House. In the Senate, on the other hand, each state had the same number of seats, regardless of population. The Senate was balanced between 11 Northern states and 11 Southern states.

In 1818, Missouri applied for statehood as a slave state. This meant that slavery would be legal there. If Missouri were to join the ranks of the slave states, those states would hold a majority of seats in the Senate. Early in 1819, New York representative James Tallmadge introduced an amendment to the statehood bill that prohibited bringing any more slaves into Missouri. Furthermore, the amendment stated, any slave born in Missouri would be emancipated, or freed, at age 25. The amended bill easily passed the House, but it was shot down in the proslavery-majority Senate.

Then, also in 1819, the free territory of Maine applied for statehood. Speaker of the House Henry Clay saw an opportunity to keep a balance of free and slave states in the Senate. He proposed that Maine and Missouri be admitted to the Union together—one as a free state and one as a slave state. He persuaded Northern congressmen to drop the amendment restricting slavery in Missouri. At the same time, he won the approval of Southern congressmen to limit slavery to the region below 36°30' north latitude, a parallel that marked the southern border of Missouri.

This agreement left the unsettled portion of the Louisiana Purchase north and west of Missouri free from slavery. The only territory in which slavery could spread was in the area that today encompasses Arkansas and Oklahoma. The proposal was passed in 1820 as the Missouri Compromise and postponed the conflict for a time.

Thirty years later, on September 9, 1850, Congress passed the Compromise of 1850. This act of legislation was created to keep Southern states from leaving the Union to form their own government. Proposed again by Clay, the compromise admitted California as a free state and ruled that the rest of the land acquired in the Mexican War—the area of present-day Utah and New Mexico—would be admitted as slave states.

At the same time, Congress passed a Fugitive Slave Act. Many slaves who escaped from their owners in the South tried to flee to the free Northern states. These fugitives often

Henry Clay (1777-1852), also called "the Great Compromiser," was the founder and leader of the Whig Party. He was successful in bringing opponents to agreement on many issues. Clay was instrumental in settling a dispute that erupted over the extension of slavery in the Missouri Territory by gaining approval for the Missouri Compromise. Lincoln admired Clay, and today Clay is known as one of the five greatest senators in American history.

used the Underground Railroad—a system of safe houses through which abolitionists helped runaway slaves to escape to freedom. Slaveholders wanted to make sure that anyone who helped a runaway slave was punished. The Fugitive Slave Act of 1850 stated that all escaped slaves must be returned to their owners. If any person in any state, slave or free, failed to turn in an escaped slave, he or she could be slapped with a hefty fine, imprisoned, or both. Many Northerners chose to ignore this law. In fact, many Northern states passed their own laws concerning runaway slaves that made the Fugitive Slave Act basically null and void. Refusal of Northern states to enforce the Fugitive Slave Act was one of the reasons that led the slave state of South Carolina finally to secede from the Union in 1860.

In 1854, Congress passed the Kansas-Nebraska Act, which overruled the Missouri Compromise. The older law had stated that any new state above 36°30' north latitude should be admitted as a free state. In contrast, the Kansas-Nebraska Act allowed each territory to decide for itself whether it wanted to be a slave state or a free state. Violence broke out in Kansas. Proslavery groups attacked the free-soil (antislavery) town of Lawrence. Radical abolitionist John Brown and his followers soon struck back, unleashing a wave of chaos and destruction that became known as Bleeding Kansas.

To make things even worse, in 1857, in the case of *Dred Scott v. Sandford*, the U.S. Supreme Court denied citizenship to all slaves, ex-slaves, and descendants of slaves. The Court also ruled that Congress no longer had the right to prohibit slavery in the territories. In response, Northern states passed a wave of personal liberty laws, declaring that no one would be denied citizenship on account of African descent. Southern states, meanwhile, passed laws to restrict slaves and free African Americans even further. In Virginia, laws restricted African Americans from entering certain parts of cities and forbade slaves from smoking, carrying canes, and standing on sidewalks.

As this social and political turbulence occurred, the Whig Party underwent a transformation. In the late 1840s, disagreements about slavery caused the party to split apart. Those Whigs who opposed slavery joined the Free-Soil Party. By 1854, the Free-Soil Party had merged with the newly formed Republican Party. This party held national interests above the rights and interests of individual states: Republicans looked to what was best for the whole country, rather than what would benefit a single state. Some Democrats who opposed slavery also broke away from their party to join the Republicans.

Lincoln always had opposed slavery. Up until this time, however, he had not viewed it as an important issue. Obviously, the times were changing, and slavery had become a problem of national importance. Lincoln began to pay more attention to slavery. He could see the day-to-day atrocities that occurred as a result of the cruel system. In a letter dated June 26, 1857, he wrote, "He who would *be* no slave, must consent to *have* no slave. Those who deny freedom to others deserve it not for themselves."

True to his character, Lincoln searched for a rational way to deal with the problems caused by slavery in a free society. Slavery in America was dangerous; it was like a ticking time bomb that ultimately could destroy the Union. At first, Lincoln thought that he had found his answer in colonization. Like his political hero, Henry Clay, Lincoln became convinced that the solution was to transport all African Americans, slave and free, to Liberia, in Africa. There, in their own colony, they could set up a government and rule themselves in freedom.

The plan was incredibly impractical. Many African Americans, born in the United States, lacked strong ties to the continent of their ancestors. They had no desire to be relocated. Moreover, Southern planters had no intentions of freeing their slaves. Slaves were a vital part of the plantation system, the chief money making enterprise of the South. Without slavery, the Southern economy would collapse. Finally, there was no way that the Northern states could pay the enormous amount of money necessary to relocate and settle millions of African

Americans in Liberia. In truth, Lincoln doubted that the scheme would work.

When the Kansas-Nebraska Act was passed, repealing the Missouri Compromise, Lincoln was appalled. He said that the news "astounded us. . . . We were thunderstruck and stunned." In Illinois, as throughout the North, there was a firestorm of opposition to the act. In August 1854, at a Whig Convention, Lincoln referred to "the great wrong and injustice of . . . the extension of slavery into free territory."

Throughout his law career, Lincoln always had had tremendous respect for the rulings of the courts and judicial due process. What troubled Lincoln most was that the chief justice of the U.S. Supreme Court had asserted that the Founding Fathers who wrote the Declaration of Independence and the Constitution never intended to include African Americans in their plans for the new nation. Lincoln believed that, with the *Dred Scott* decision, the Supreme Court had taken a hammer to the plain and unmistakable language of the Declaration, a document sacred to all Americans. In a speech that he gave in Springfield, Illinois, on June 26, 1857, Lincoln said,

> I think the authors of [the Declaration of Independence] intended to include all men, but they did not intend to declare all men equal in all respects. They did not mean to say that all were equal in color, size, intellect, moral development, or social capacity. They defined with tolerable distinctness, in what respects they did consider all men created equal—equal in "certain inalienable rights, among which are life, liberty, and the pursuit of happiness." This they said, and this they meant.

In Lincoln's mind, the courts had misinterpreted the Declaration and, as a result, had torn it apart. The Supreme Court had so grossly distorted this document fundamental to American liberty, Lincoln believed, that if the framers were to rise from their graves they would scarcely recognize the Declaration at all. Lincoln's faith in the judicial system was shaken so much that he never again gave credence to the rulings of the U.S. Supreme Court.

In 1856 and 1858, Lincoln ran for the U.S. Senate. He lost both times. After being nominated by the Republican Party in 1858, he gave one of his most memorable acceptance speeches. "A house divided against itself cannot stand," he said. "I believe

DRED SCOTT VS. SANDFORD

The *Dred Scott* case made Lincoln rethink his position on the judicial system. Dred Scott was a slave who was born in Virigina and moved with his owner to free Illinois and, later, to free Wisconsin. When the slaveholder moved back to the slave state of Missouri, Scott sued for his freedom on the grounds that he had lived in a free state. Based on previous cases, if a slave returned to Missouri, as Scott had done, after living in a free state or territory, that slave was entitled to freedom. The premise was, "Once free, always free." In the lower courts, consistent with past rulings, Scott was declared free. Seeking a reversal, Scott's owner appealed the case to the Missouri Supreme Court. Claiming that times had changed, the Missouri Supreme Court reversed the decision of the lower court. Scott, the jurists said, was still a slave. When Scott's lawyers appealed his case to the United States Supreme Court, that highest court in the land upheld the ruling of the Missouri Supreme Court. Lincoln firmly believed that, in this case, the Supreme Courts of Missouri and the United States were wrong.

the government cannot endure, permanently half *slave* and half *free*. I do not expect the Union to be *dissolved*—I do not expect the house to *fall*—but I *do* expect it will cease to be divided. It will become *all* one thing, or *all* the other." In the 1858 race for the Illinois Senate seat, Lincoln challenged Democrat Stephen A. Douglas, who was up for reelection.

By the time of his 1854 campaign, Lincoln had built up quite a political reputation. He was a favorite among Midwestern Republicans. His clear, articulate presentation of the issues won over the educated, upper-class voters, and his homespun humor appealed to the country folk. Referring to the Declaration of Independence, he asserted that slavery was inconsistent with human rights and natural law. The new territories, he believed, should be kept free of slavery.

During the campaign, both Lincoln and Douglas traveled around the state, delivering speeches and responding to each other's points. In July, Lincoln suggested that the two candidates meet face-to-face for a formal debate, something that was unusual at the time. Reluctantly, Douglas accepted. Throughout the late summer, they met at seven different towns. They engaged in a deeper-than-usual, intellectual discussion of slavery. During the debates, Lincoln tried to emphasize the ways that a continued tolerance of slavery could bring only violence and destruction to the Union. Douglas argued that the best course was to keep things as they were at present. In the end, Douglas won the election, but only by eight votes.

The 1858 debates were widely covered and well reported in newspapers across the country. Lincoln's performance in these debates catapulted him to political stardom throughout the free states and put him in a leadership position within the Republican Party. When Lincoln and Douglas met again, it was in a race for the presidency. Already, there were whispers about states threatening to secede from the Union if Lincoln were elected president. Civil war sat on the doorstep of every American home.

"LIBERTY *AND* UNION"

Slavery: yes or no? The question was a crucial one. In the South, the economy was based on agriculture. Large plantations produced such cash crops as cotton, tobacco, and sugarcane to export to the Northern states and to Europe. The South depended on the North for manufactured goods, financial services, and businesses essential to trade. The agricultural economy of the South relied heavily on the unpaid labor of nearly 4 million enslaved African Americans. Although the slaveholding planters represented only a small percentage of the South's total population, they dominated Southern politics and society. Simply, the plantations' slave workforces were the largest fixed assets in the South. Without slave labor, wealthy plantation owners would not be able to operate their large farms. Without slavery, the Southern economy would crumble. Whether right or wrong, no white Southerner wanted to lose his or her way of life. For this reason, the Southerners were stubborn. They were willing to fight to the death for their beliefs. Northerners, most of whose livelihoods did not depend on slavery, focused on the moral side of the issue. They believed that all Americans, black and white, had the right to freedom.

The presidential election of 1860 became the most spectacular campaign of the century. It was a four-candidate race to the finish line. The Democratic Party split into Northern and Southern factions. In the South, Democrats endorsed John C. Breckinridge of Kentucky. The Northern Democrats chose Lincoln's great adversary, Stephen A. Douglas. The newly formed Constitutional Union Party, which was made up of conservative former Whigs and men dissatisfied with the other parties, selected John Bell of Tennessee as their candidate.

The Republican Party rallied around Abraham Lincoln—the "rail splitter" from the Midwest. At this point, the Republican platform opposed the further expansion of slavery into western territories. Although Lincoln believed that slavery was morally wrong, he did not propose to abolish slavery in the Southern

When Lincoln was inaugurated on March 4, 1861 (*shown above*), the atmosphere was tense with rumors of plots to kill or carry Lincoln off before he could take office. Sharpshooters had orders to shoot anyone in the crowd moving toward Lincoln's carriage, and Lieutenant General Winfield Scott, who also received threats, ordered soldiers to surround the carriage as it traveled to the Capitol.

states. His main objective was to preserve the Union. He knew that if slavery were to be outlawed in every state, the South would break away from the North. Lincoln wanted to keep the United States together. He once told Billy Herndon that Daniel Webster's brilliant 1830 speech, in which Webster concluded,

"Liberty *and* Union, now and forever, one and inseparable," was the best speech ever delivered.

At the same time, Lincoln scolded the South for its threats of secession. Southerners had gone so far as to blame the North for the growing conflict. If the South left the Union, these Southerners claimed, it would be the Northerners' fault. During a speech at Cooper Union in Manhattan on the night of February 27, 1860, Lincoln poked fun at this ridiculous argument. "That is cool," Lincoln remarked. "A highwayman holds a pistol to my ear, and mutters through his teeth, 'Stand and deliver, or I shall kill you, and then you will be a murderer!'" This speech propelled Lincoln to even greater popularity. Victory seemed certain.

Ultimately, the Democratic split handed the election to Lincoln. At about two o' clock in the morning on November 7, 1860, Lincoln learned he had clinched the presidency. He had been waiting at the telegraph office for the results. When the official tally finally was registered, Lincoln received 1,866,452 votes to Douglas's 1,346,957. Breckinridge tallied 849,781 votes, and Bell gained 588,879. With less than 40 percent of the popular vote, Lincoln won 180 of the 303 electoral votes. Douglas finished with just 12 electoral votes. When news of Lincoln's victory reached the cities and towns of the Northeast, celebrations erupted in the streets. There were boisterous hurrahs, a gun salute for each of the free states, and hearty cheers for "Honest Old Abe," president of the United States.

In Springfield, Lincoln stepped out of the telegraph office into a brisk, Midwestern wind. As he rode through the streets on his way home, the dark sky blanketed him like a heavy cloak. Victory seemed almost sinister. That night, he tossed in his bed, getting little sleep. "I then felt as I never had before," he remembered, "the responsibility that was upon me."

The Bloody War

By March 1861, when Lincoln was inaugurated, seven Southern states had seceded from the Union. These seven states—South Carolina, Mississippi, Florida, Alabama, Georgia, Louisiana, and Texas—formed a new country, the Confederate States of America, and elected Jefferson Davis as their president.

In his inaugural address, President Lincoln declared that secession was illegal. The Union fully intended to keep its possessions in the South. In essence, the Union would not recognize the Confederacy as an independent country. Undoubtedly, Lincoln recalled the statements he had made nearly a decade earlier, asserting that every state was entitled to break away and form its own government. Such contradictions mattered little now, however. He had changed his mind, and he needed to do everything in his power to preserve the Union and avoid a war.

If the upholding of slavery would have saved the Union, Lincoln probably would have rethought his position, even if to do so would have meant to go against his personal beliefs. Lincoln knew, however, that the acceptance of slavery was not the solution. There was nothing he could do to change the minds of Southerners. The battle lines were drawn.

On April 12, 1861, the Union attempted to resupply Fort Sumter in Charleston harbor, in Confederate South Carolina. Confederate troops at the fort believed that this territory belonged to the Confederacy, not the Union. When Union troops refused to give up the fort, Confederate troops opened fire. After three days, the Rebels finally surrendered to the Union soldiers. What was hailed as a victory in the North was looked on with horror across the South. In response to the battle, the states of Virginia, Arkansas, North Carolina, and Tennessee seceded from the Union to join the Confederacy. The bloodiest war in American history had begun.

In 1861, neither the North nor the South was prepared to wage war. At a glance, the North, with a population of 22 million, had greater military potential. The South's population was 9 million, but that included the nearly 4 million African-American slaves. The North possessed other clear advantages, such as money and credit, factories for food and ammunition production, mineral resources, and better transportation systems. The South was hampered by a lack of food supplies, clothing, medicine, and heavy artillery. Even with superior manpower and resources, however, the North could not achieve the quick victory that it had at first expected. Lincoln needed time to build, train, and equip a massive fighting force. In the South, the Confederates had a strong military command; the Rebel army boasted such experienced officers as General Robert E. Lee. Through painful trial and error, Lincoln finally found comparable leaders in Ulysses S. Grant and William T. Sherman.

Beyond a highly trained military, the Confederacy had other advantages. The war would be fought on familiar

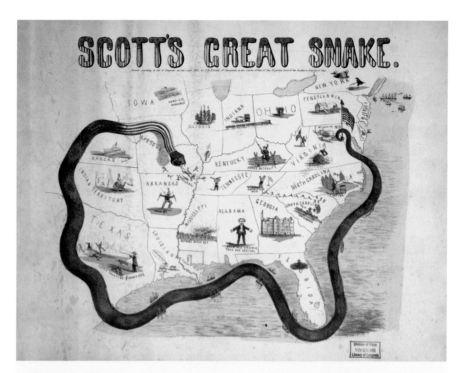

The Anaconda Plan *(above)*, proposed by General Winfield Scott, called for the blockade of Southern ports and an advance of about 80,000 Union soldiers down the Mississippi River to cut the South in two. On a map, it looks like a snake coiling around its victim, giving the plan its name. Civil War historians often credit the Anaconda Plan with guiding Lincoln's strategy throughout the war.

Southern terrain. If the South could keep Union soldiers in the field until they lost the will to fight, the Confederacy would win the war. The Union forces had to attack on a broad front and sustain long distances of communication and supply; the South merely had to defend itself.

As president, Lincoln had two possible military strategies to consider. The Union Army could make a direct, overland march to the Confederate capital in Richmond, Virginia. If Union soldiers could capture Richmond, the loss of the capital might discourage the South and bring the war to a rapid close. Lincoln's military advisors counseled him to follow another route, however. It was called the "Anaconda Plan" and was devised by General Winfield Scott. This strategy called for placing a naval blockade around the Confederacy to prevent supplies from arriving from Europe. Following the blockade, Union soldiers would invade the Mississippi River Valley, thereby cutting the Confederacy in two and forcing it to fall on itself. Lincoln implemented the Anaconda Plan, the name of which came from a giant snake that wraps itself around its prey and then squeezes the life from it.

In the South, Confederate leaders also disagreed about the most effective strategy. The president of the Confederate States of America, Jefferson Davis, thought in terms of a defensive war; he wanted to wear down the North while attracting foreign sympathy and support. With such a long stretch of exposed border between the North and the South, however, such a strategy seemed unrealistic. An alternate plan called for an offensive strike into the North before the Union had time to build up its army and supplies. Most Southerners believed that the longer the war dragged on, the less chance the Confederacy had to win.

UNION BLUNDERS

When the Civil War began, both sides were confident of an early victory. In May 1861, Union troops crossed the Potomac River and recaptured Alexandria, Virginia. Union officer Elmer Ellsworth spotted a Confederate flag waving above a hotel—a flag that President Lincoln could see from the White House with a spyglass. Flushed with victory, Ellsworth dashed up the front steps of the hotel to yank the flag down. The hotel-keeper shot and killed the young officer on his way back down the steps. Ellsworth's death deeply grieved Lincoln, who had treated the young man as a son.

Up until this point, Lincoln had put off making a Union advance. Now, filled with fire, he called for action. The plans were simple and direct. Believing that Confederate general Pierre G.T. Beauregard had about 35,000 men at Manassas

Junction, Virginia, Lincoln ordered a swift attack on the Confederates before they could be reinforced. The junction was a key railroad center about 30 miles southwest of Washington, D.C. Union general Irvin McDowell was not ready to move until a week later. It proved to be a costly delay. By that time, Confederate reinforcements had arrived.

On July 21, Confederate troops won a resounding victory at Manassas in the First Battle of Bull Run. Although it was not a crucial loss strategically, it was a humiliating setback for the North. The Union had to abandon all hopes for a 90-day war and began to raise money for a mightier army. In the Confederacy, Bull Run puffed up the army with overconfidence that hindered its preparations for the long conflict that lay ahead.

Assuming responsibility for the defeat at Bull Run, Lincoln immediately worked to remedy the situation. To boost morale, he visited the fortification around Washington and assured the troops there that they would be equipped with all needed supplies. At the same time, he realized that the Union needed a better commanding general. He replaced General Irvin McDowell with General George B. McClellan as commander of the forces around Washington. An able administrator and drillmaster, McClellan reorganized the Army of the Potomac. The 34-year-old general was popular with the troops. He was also conceited and arrogant, however, and he had a tendency to overestimate the enemy. His excessive caution and his pompous personality quickly wore out Lincoln's patience.

As McClellan worked to build up a superior army, Lincoln spent a few enjoyable months with his family in their new home—the White House. At first, the children were a bit overwhelmed by the 31-room mansion. Their entire house in Springfield would have fit into the East Room. Willie and Tad were the first children ever to live in the White House. On many afternoons, they played with their pet goats, Nanko and Nanny. One day, Tad harnessed Nanko to a chair, which became his sled. With a whoop, he and Nanko charged through the East

Room, where a reception was under way. Nanko pulled Tad around the room, past the trouser legs and hoop skirts of the well-dressed guests, and finally out the door again. On some evenings, Lincoln played with his sons, teasing them and wrestling with them. Such moments were rare, however. During his time in the White House, Lincoln worked harder than almost any other American president.

In early 1862, tragedy once again struck the Lincoln family. At the beginning of February, Willie fell ill with typhoid fever. On February 20, he died. Distraught on losing a second son, both parents were overcome with grief. Mary never fully recovered from the loss. In tears, Abe choked out these broken words: "He was too good for this earth—but then we loved him so."

Throughout much of 1861, the war was at a stalemate. The North scored some critical successes in securing the border states of Maryland, Delaware, Kentucky, and Missouri. Maryland was especially important because of its location surrounding Washington, D.C. Additionally, a Baltimore, Maryland, railroad station was a key link to the Midwest. In order to make sure that Maryland stayed loyal to the Union, federal troops occupied Baltimore and imposed martial law.

Like Maryland, Kentucky and Missouri were critical from a strategic standpoint. These states controlled the approaches to the Mississippi, Tennessee, and Cumberland River valleys, through which Union forces could bring the war to the Confederate heartland. Originally, Kentucky had tried to remain neutral. In September 1861, however, Confederate troops crossed the Kentucky border. Faced with this invasion, many Kentuckians joined the Union cause. In Missouri, Union troops drove the pro-Confederate governor into exile. In parts of Virginia, people had mixed feelings about the war. The western counties of the state rejected the order of secession. They formed their own provisional government and, in 1863, were admitted into the Union as the new state of West Virginia.

In the spring of 1862, McClellan and his army were ready to take the offensive. They implemented the strategy of an overland march to Richmond. McClellan moved his army of 100,000 men onto the peninsula between the James and York rivers. From there, southeast of Richmond, the Union troops began their advance toward the Confederate capital. On May 31 and June 1, the Union and Confederate armies clashed in the Battle of Seven Pines (also called the Battle for Fair Oaks).

Early on, McClellan's army repelled the Confederate forces. In the Confederate camp, General Lee stepped up to replace a wounded General Joseph Johnston as commander of the Army of Northern Virginia. By June, the Union Army had inched closer to Richmond. Overly cautious as usual, McClellan decided to wait for reinforcements before attacking. Meanwhile, Thomas "Stonewall" Jackson was marching his army up the Shenandoah Valley and crossing the Potomac. Jackson's plan was to relieve pressure on Richmond, and it worked.

Worried about an attack on Washington, President Lincoln refused to send McClellan his reinforcements. By this time, however, Jackson already had turned back from an approach on Washington and was on his way to join forces with General Lee. Lee and Jackson marched an army of 85,000 men against the Union forces near Richmond. From June 25 to July 1, the battle dragged on, with no apparent victor. Fearing that the Union forces were vastly outnumbered, McClellan ordered a retreat to the James River.

Severely disappointed in McClellan, Lincoln named Major General Henry Halleck as the new general in chief of all the Union armies. McClellan stayed in command of the Army of the Potomac, but Lincoln called General John Pope from the western front to head a new army to "check" Jackson. Pope's term as commander was short-lived, however. On August 30, the Second Battle of Bull Run brought another tragic Union defeat. The combined forces of Lee, Jackson, and General James Longstreet inflicted heavy casualties on the Union Army

Here, Lincoln meets with Major General George B. McClellan at Antietam on October 3, 1862. The Battle of Antietam was the Civil War's bloodiest single day of battle. Lincoln was disappointed that McClellan had not crushed General Lee and ordered McClellan's removal on November 5. Still, this battle is considered a turning point of the war because it led to Lincoln's issue of the Emancipation Proclamation and the end of Lee's strategic campaign.

and sent it retreating back to Washington. There, Pope was promptly relieved of his command.

In September 1862, Lee startled the North by invading Maryland with about 50,000 troops. He hoped to strike a blow at Union morale. In addition, he believed that a victory on Union soil might encourage foreign countries to come to the aid of the Confederacy. McClellan, with an army of 90,000 men, moved to check Lee's advance. On September 17, in the bloody Battle of Antietam, about 12,000 Union soldiers and 12,700 Confederate soldiers were killed or wounded. The Union forces managed to push Lee's army back to Virginia but failed to cut off his retreat. Frustrated, Lincoln removed General McClellan from command and replaced him with General Ambrose Burnside.

By late 1862, the Army of the Potomac had resumed its offensive march toward Richmond. On December 13, however, Burnside made an unwise decision for the Union forces. He chose to challenge Lee's nearly impenetrable defenses around Fredericksburg, Virginia, on the Rappahannok River. The attack turned into yet another Union disaster. The Northern forces suffered more than 10,000 killed or wounded, and the Union troops were forced, again, to retreat to Washington.

Despite recurring failures in the East, the Union forces were not entirely thwarted. The Union Army waged war on another front, in the West. With superb commanders and military maneuvers, the North's successes in the West offered a shimmer of hope for a Union victory.

THE WESTERN CAMPAIGN

In the West, the Union was far more successful. On this front, the Union's objective was to gain control of the Mississippi Valley, thereby splitting the Confederacy in two and cutting off the flow of supplies from Louisiana, Texas, and Arkansas. In early 1862, General Ulysses S. Grant, with the support of a fleet of ironclad ships, captured Fort Henry in Tennessee, on the Tennessee River. Later, his fleet captured Fort Donelson, on the Cumberland River, along with 16,000 Confederate troops. His victories opened a clear path down the Mississippi.

Meanwhile, west of the Mississippi, Union troops defeated Confederate forces at Pea Ridge, Arkansas, in a battle fought from March 6 to 8. This victory ended the threat of a Confederate invasion of Missouri. Dropping back from its position around Nashville, the Confederate Army in northern Tennessee retreated southward to Mississippi. There, the Confederates tried to establish a new line of defense. Grant brought an abrupt halt to the advance at Shiloh, Tennessee, and waited to be reinforced by an army under the command of General Don Carlos Buell. The Confederate Army was hungry for a chance at victory. Under General Albert S. Johnston, the Rebels staged a nearly successful surprise attack on April 6. The reinforcement of Buell's men arrived in the nick of time, however, and the combined Union forces repelled the attack, forcing the Confederate Army to retreat. On May 30, in Corinth, Mississippi, a railroad center critical to the Southern defenses fell to Union troops. By early June, Union forces had overrun most of western and eastern Tennessee and controlled the Mississippi River Valley as far south as Memphis.

At the same time that General Grant was pushing southward, Union forces were moving up the Mississippi from the south. In April, a naval squadron commanded by Captain David G. Farragut penetrated Confederate defenses at the mouth of the Mississippi and forced the surrender of New Orleans. On May 1, Union troops under General Benjamin Butler moved into New Orleans, the Confederacy's largest city and principal port. Toward the end of 1862, Grant secured his position along the Mississippi. Lincoln ordered Buell to attack Chattanooga, Tennessee. There, Buell's army fought Confederate forces, but without a certain winner. In December, General William Rosecrans, who replaced Buell, engaged in the three-day Battle of Murfreesboro. On the banks of the Stones River, Union soldiers confronted Confederate troops under General Braxton Bragg and ultimately forced a Confederate retreat.

Meanwhile, General Grant prepared for an assault on Vicksburg, Mississippi, the last remaining Confederate stronghold in the West. Perched high on the bluffs overlooking the Mississippi River, Vicksburg was considered an invincible fortress. As the Confederates predicted, the city was able to

Here, Lincoln meets with his cabinet on July 22, 1862, for the first draft of the reading of the preliminary Emancipation Proclamation. Pictured is *(left to right)* Edwin Stanton, Salmon Chase, Lincoln, Gideon Welles, Caleb B. Smith, William Seward, Montgomery Blair, and Edward Bates.

withstand Union attacks. Bogged down by the rugged terrain that protected the city, Grant's army finally retreated.

About this time, Lincoln was drafting a document that would become one of the most important and influential executive orders in U.S. history. The Emancipation Proclamation consisted of two orders. Issued on September 22, 1862, the first order declared the freedom of all slaves in any Confederate state that did not return to Union control by January 1, 1863. The second order—issued on January 1, 1863—named the specific states to which the proclamation applied. Lincoln issued the executive order by his authority as commander in chief of the army and Navy under Article II, Section 2 of the U.S. Constitution.

THE EMANCIPATION PROCLAMATION

Whereas on the 22nd day of September, in the year of our Lord one thousand eight hundred sixty-two, a proclamation was issued by the president of the United States, containing, among other things, the following:

"That on the 1st day of January, in the year of our Lord one thousand eight hundred sixty-three, all persons held as slaves within any State, or designated part of a State the people whereof shall then be in rebellion against the United States, shall be then, thenceforward, and forever free; and the executive government of the United States, including the military and naval authority thereof, will recognize and maintain the freedom of such persons and will do no act or acts to repress such persons, or any of them, in any efforts they may make for their actual freedom.

"That the executive will on the 1st day of January aforesaid, by proclamation, designate the States and parts of States, if any, in which the people thereof, respectively, shall then be in rebellion against the United States; and the fact that any State or the people thereof shall on that day be in good faith represented in the Congress of the United States by members chosen thereto at elections wherein a majority of the qualified voters of such State shall have participated, shall in the absence of strong countervailing testimony, be deemed conclusive evidence that such State and the people thereof are not then in rebellion against the United States."

Now, therefore, I, Abraham Lincoln, President of the United States, by virtue of the power in me vested as

(continues)

Widely attacked at the time, the Emancipation Proclamation freed only slaves over which the Union had no power. Also, it committed the Union to ending slavery, which

(continued)

Commander-in-Chief of the Army and Navy of the United States in time of actual armed rebellion against the authority and government of the United States, and as a fit and necessary war measure for repressing said rebellion, do, on this first day of January, in the year of our Lord one thousand eight hundred sixty-three, and in accordance with my purpose so to do, publicly proclaimed for the full period of one hundred days from the first day above mentioned, order and designate as the States, and parts of States wherein the people thereof, respectively, are this day in rebellion against the United States, the following, to wit:

Arkansas, Texas, Louisiana (except the parishes of St. Bernard, Plaquemines, Jefferson, St. John, St. Charles, St. James, Ascension, Assumption, Terre Bonne, Lafourche, St. Mary, St. Martin, and Orleans, including the city of New Orleans), Mississippi, Alabama, Florida, Georgia, South Carolina, North Carolina, and Virginia (except the forty-eight counties designated as West Virginia, and also the counties of Berkeley, Accomac, Northhampton, Elizabeth City, York, Princess Ann, and Norfolk, including the cities of Norfolk and Portsmouth), and which excepted parts are for the present left precisely as if this proclamation were not issued.

And by virtue of the power and for the purpose aforesaid, I do order and declare that all persons held as slaves within said designated States and parts of States

was still a controversial issue in the North. The proclamation did not free slaves of the border states—including Kentucky, Missouri, Maryland, Delaware, and West Virginia—or any

are, and henceforward shall be, free; and that the executive government of the United States, including the military and naval authorities thereof, will recognize and maintain the freedom of said persons.

And I hereby enjoin upon the people so declared to be free to abstain from all violence, unless in necessary self-defense; and I recommend to them that, in all cases when allowed, they labor faithfully for reasonable wages.

And I further declare and make known that such persons of suitable condition will be received into the armed service of the United States to garrison forts, positions, stations, and other places, and to man vessels of all sorts in said service.

And upon this act, sincerely believed to be an act of justice, warranted by the Constitution upon military necessity, I invoke the considerate judgment of mankind and the gracious favor of Almighty God.

In witness whereof, I have hereunto set my hand, and caused the seal of the United States to be affixed.

Done at the city of Washington, this first day of January, in the year of our Lord one thousand eight hundred [L.S.] sixty-three, and of the independence of the United States of America the eighty-seventh.

By the President:
    Abraham Lincoln

William H. Seward, Secretary of State

Southern state or part of a Southern state already under Union control. Hearing about the proclamation, thousands of slaves escaped Confederate states and fled to Union lines. The proclamation was immediately denounced by Copperhead Democrats, a group of Democrats who opposed the war and tolerated both secession and slavery. In the 1862 elections, it became a campaign issue, and the Democrats gained 28 seats in the House, as well as the governorship of New York. Many War Democrats, who had supported Lincoln's goal of saving the Union, were also reluctant to support emancipation. At the same time, the proclamation solidified Lincoln's support among the rapidly growing abolitionist segment of the Republican Party and ensured his renomination in 1864.

As Lincoln hoped, the proclamation turned foreign popular opinion in favor of the Union for its new commitment to end slavery, ending the Confederacy's hopes of gaining recognition and support from Great Britain. Prior to Lincoln's decree, Great Britain's actions had favored the Confederacy, especially in the building of warships such as the CSS *Alabama* and CSS *Florida*. Great Britain and France, however, had both already abolished slavery. If these countries were to support the Confederacy, they would be supporting slavery. In the end, the Emancipation Proclamation did more for the Union and diplomacy than all its former victories.

TURNING POINT

On January 26, 1863, General Joseph "Fighting Joe" Hooker took over as commander of the Army of the Potomac. He promised to reverse the string of Union defeats in the East. In April 1863, at the head of an army 130,000 strong, he prepared to challenge Lee and his army of 60,000 near Fredericksburg, Virginia. While holding Lee at Fredericksburg, Hooker dispatched a group of soldiers to attack the Confederate flank. Hesitant to use his reserves at a critical moment, Hooker chose to withdraw from his defensive position at Chancellorsville,

Virginia. During this moment of hesitation, the combined forces of Lee and Jackson bombarded Hooker's army and forced them to retreat. The battle proved just as costly for the South as for the North, however. Lee lost almost one-fifth of his men, as well as the brilliant general Stonewall Jackson. Lincoln was greatly disturbed by the crushing defeat. With a face pale and ghostlike, he paced back and forth, exclaiming, "What will the country say!"

Elated with his victory, Lee seized the moment. He marched his army into Northern territory. Lee hoped that this move would relieve pressure on the weary Confederate forces in the West and persuade a war-worn North to negotiate peace. In June, a Confederate army of 75,000 advanced through the Shenandoah Valley into southern Pennsylvania. The Army of the Potomac, now commanded by George Meade, moved to halt Lee's march. On July 1, 1863, these two enormous armies converged at the small town of Gettysburg, Pennsylvania. The ensuing battle became a turning point in the war. Union forces managed to secure a strategic position on high ground south of Gettysburg. Lee's army tried to attack the position from various points, but his soldiers were repeatedly thrown back. In an intense artillery duel, Lee ordered division commander George E. Pickett to charge the center of the Union line at Cemetery Ridge. The attack failed. Suffering serious casualties, Lee turned back, but his retreat was blocked by the flooded Potomac River.

Again, much to Lincoln's annoyance, Meade failed to exploit Lee's predicament, and the tattered Confederate army eventually retreated into northern Virginia. Still, Lincoln had waited anxiously for a victory in the East. The news from Gettysburg was a taste of sweet relief for the exhausted president. As the war dragged on, Lincoln's face grew old and worn: There were dark bags beneath his sunken eyes, and the never-ending anxiety that haunted him left deep creases in his forehead. Perhaps now, after the Union victory at Gettysburg, the war was nearing its end.

Here, Lincoln delivers the Gettysburg Address. At the time, anti-Lincoln sentiment was growing and Copperhead Democrats were calling for his ouster in order to end the war. Lincoln realized that he needed to say something to revive the Union's spirits to the war efforts. Scheduled to be delivered sixth in order of other presentations that day, the Gettysburg Address is one of the most quoted speeches in history.

On the western front, Grant had rallied his forces for a renewed attempt to capture Vicksburg. In April 1863, with backup from Union gunboats and supply ships, Grant had set up his army on the south side of the city. In a series of bold maneuvers, he took the Rebels by surprise and divided the Confederate defenders. He split and separated their forces in order to weaken them. By mid May, Union forces had reached

Vicksburg. At the end of a 47-day siege during which many Vicksburg residents sought refuge in caves to escape the constant battery of Grant's guns, the city fell into Union hands. The Union had achieved its goal in the West: It had bisected the Confederacy.

With the Mississippi secured, Lincoln decided that it was time to drive the Confederate Army out of eastern Tennessee. If Rebel forces could be driven out of the way there, the Union Army could make a clear sweep into Georgia. The Union advance was stopped, however, when the Northern force encountered a reinforced Confederate army of 70,000 men, led by General Bragg. On September 19 and 20, the Confederates pummeled the Union troops in the Battle of Chickamauga, forcing them to retreat to Chattanooga.

General Grant was now in full command of the Union forces. He replaced a floundering General Rosecrans with George Thomas and headed for Chattanooga with his Army of Tennessee. During the three-day Battle of Chattanooga, from November 23 to 25, the Union forces dislodged the Rebels and forced them into a chaotic retreat. By the end of 1863, the war had turned in the Union's favor. After his defeat at Gettysburg, Lee was unable to mount a successful offensive in the North. In the West, the Union Army had divided the Confederacy in two. Now, the triumph at Chattanooga opened the way for a march into Alabama and Georgia.

In Grant, Lincoln had finally found a general he could count on. He appointed Grant commander in chief of all Union forces. After demonstrating his military prowess in the West, Grant wanted to use the North's great manpower and superior industry to wear down the enemy. He also designed a strategy that would tighten the Union's stranglehold on the Confederacy. Commanded by Grant and Meade, the Army of the Potomac would engage Lee in battle in northern Virginia and move on to Richmond. Meanwhile, another army, led by William T. Sherman, would march south from Chattanooga into Georgia and capture Atlanta. Yet another army, under Philip Sheridan, would lay siege to the Shenandoah Valley, thereby depriving Lee's forces of much-needed food and supplies.

In late March 1864, the Army of the Potomac—155,000 strong—began its Wilderness Campaign. The army marched until it reached a deserted area near Chancellorsville, Virginia, that was known as the Wilderness. There, the Union forces faced Lee's smaller army of 62,000. During a two-day battle, on May 5 and 6, North and South fought in the thicket of a dense forest. Both sides suffered heavy casualties, and no clear winner emerged. Unlike his predecessors, however, Grant pushed on, determined to keep full pressure on the enemy.

At Spotsylvania Courthouse, from May 8 to 12, the two sides clashed again, once more without a retreat. Lee held off an attack at Cold Harbor, just north of Richmond. Instead of pushing on to Richmond, Grant chose another strategic move. He bypassed the Confederate capital, crossed the James River, and charged Petersburg, Virginia, a railroad center vital to Richmond's supply line. His attempt to sever Richmond's lifeline failed, however, when he met a reinforced Confederate army. On June 20, Grant ordered another attack, but, once again, the Rebel defenders held firm. For the next nine months, Grant made several attempts to seize the city; one of those attempts became known as the Battle of the Crater. Each time, the Union forces were beaten back, bringing the offensive operation in Virginia to a temporary halt.

During the summer of 1864, General Sherman led 90,000 Union troops toward Atlanta. Along the way, the Rebels tried unsuccessfully to stop him, including in a battle at Kennesaw Mountain. Sherman managed to cut off Atlanta's main supply line, and by September 1, the Confederate troops had abandoned the city.

Northerners, thrilled to hear of Union successes, elected Lincoln to a second term in November. After the loss of Atlanta, Confederate general John Bell Hood tried to weaken

Sherman's extensive supply line. He boldly marched his troops into Tennessee, assuming that Sherman would follow to protect Chattanooga. Instead, Sherman dispatched a part of his force to counter Hood and prepared the rest of his men to march across Georgia to Savannah. On November 30, 1864, Hood's army battled Sherman's dispatched troops at Franklin, Tennessee. The Rebels' attempts to charge the Union line failed, however. On December 15, Hood made another attack, in the Battle of Nashville. The following day, Union troops delivered the final, crushing blow. They defeated Hood and brought an end to Confederate resistance in the West.

On November 15, 1864, Sherman began his famous March to the Sea. His army had battled its way through northern Georgia, 100 miles to Atlanta. On September 7, Atlanta had fallen to the Union forces. Now, in November, Sherman's men left the second-most-important Southern city ransacked and in flames. The Union Army marched on, with the flickering glow of Atlanta as a backdrop. On the 60-mile trek to Savannah, the soldiers destroyed everything in their path. They gutted plantation houses and other buildings, burned crops, and slaughtered livestock. Sherman's strategy was to wage a devastating psychological war, which he called "hard war." Modern historians call it "total war."

Shortly before Christmas, Savannah fell. Sherman continued his path of fiery destruction northward, into the Carolinas and Alabama. One by one, Southern cities surrendered and were burned: Mobile, Selma, and Montgomery, Alabama, all fell to Sherman's army in April 1865. In Virginia, General Grant launched a final assault on Lee's army. At last, Union forces seized the railroad that supplied Richmond. Forced to flee from Petersburg and Richmond, Lee retreated westward, hoping to join General Johnston in North Carolina. Grant headed off his escape. On Palm Sunday, April 9, 1865, Lee surrendered to Grant at Appomattox Courthouse, in Virginia.

He Belongs
to the Ages

After Lee's downfall, the remaining Confederate armies quickly collapsed one after another, like dominoes. At dawn on April 10 in Washington, the sound of 500 cannon blasts broke the news of victory to the entire capital. All day, the nation celebrated. Outside the White House, bands played music and people cheered. That afternoon, Lincoln stepped out to say a few words. He then asked the band to play "Dixie"—one of his favorite songs. Inviting the South back into the Union like a father welcomes home a lost child, he told the crowd that it was one of the best tunes he had ever heard. With his classic sense of humor, he joked that the song was a lawful prize, since the Union had fairly captured it.

In physical devastation and loss of human life, the Civil War was the costliest war in the history of America. At the end, out

THE "RAIL SPLITTER" AT WORK REPAIRING THE UNION.

Discussions about how to repair the Union began before the end of the Civil War. Some officials favored harsh treatment of states that seceded from the Union, while Lincoln wanted to reunite the nation as painlessly and quickly as possible. This political cartoon of Andrew Johnson and Abe Lincoln entitled "The Rail Splitter at Work Repairing the Union" shows them attempting to sew the Union back together by needle and thread.

of a nation of 35 million people, 620,000 soldiers died, and at least that many more were wounded. Out of the North, 364,000 soldiers were killed—nearly one out of every five Union soldiers. The South suffered 258,000 killed—nearly one of every four Confederate soldiers. More men died of disease and sickness than on the battlefield, however. Devastation of property was largely limited to the South, where most of the battles took place. Huge chunks of Richmond, Charleston, Atlanta, Mobile, and Vicksburg lay in charred ruins. Proud plantations had been reduced to smoldering skeletons of mansions, barns, and, fields. More than $4 billion worth of property had been wiped out, including the loss of slaves to freedom.

With the Civil War over, a daunting task lay ahead for President Lincoln. He had succeeded in preserving the Union, but now it had to be pieced back together, mended, thread by thread. A sense of unity had to be restored. The government needed to be reestablished in the South. And 4 million slaves had to be integrated into American society. This reconstruction would cause just as much conflict and bitterness as the war itself.

THE HOMESTEAD ACT OF 1862

On May 20, Lincoln signed the Federal Homestead Act of 1862. At the time of signing, 11 states had already left the Union. Prior to secession, the distribution of government lands had been a hotly debated issue. Southern states worried that rapid settlement of western territories would lead to new states populated by small farmers who opposed slavery. In 1852, 1854, and 1859, the House of Representatives passed homestead legislation, but it was defeated in the Senate. In 1860, a homestead bill providing federal land grants to western settlers passed Congress only to be vetoed by President James Buchanan. When Southern states left the Union, the issue of slavery went with them. Finally, a Homestead Act could be passed and signed into law with no resistance from the Southern delegates.

The new law established a three-part homestead acquisition process: submitting an application, improving the land, and filing for a deed of title. Any U.S. citizen, or intended citizen, who had never borne arms against the United States could file an application and lay claim to 160 acres of surveyed government land. For the next 5 years, the homesteader had to live on and improve the land by building a 12-foot-by-14-foot house and growing crops. After 5 years, the homesteader could then file for a deed of title. Valid claims were granted a deed of title to the land, free and clear, except for a small registration fee. A title could also be acquired after a 6-month residency and lesser improvements, provided the homesteader paid the government $1.25 per acre. One of the first homesteaders was Daniel Freeman and his wife, Agnes. Freeman, a Union scout, joined the post-Civil War wave of homesteaders who mainly traveled from the Ohio and Mississippi valleys. Later, European immigrants were enticed by railroad companies selling off millions of acres of land grants, at a price. By 1900, homesteaders had filed 600,000 claims for 80 million acres.

SUSPENSION OF HABEAS CORPUS

During spring 1861, riots exploded in various cities across the nation. At the same time, the border slave state of Maryland threatened to secede from the Union, leaving the nation's capital, Washington, D.C., surrounded by hostile territory. In response, on April 27, 1861, President Lincoln suspended habeas corpus in some parts of the Union, including Maryland. It was one of nine proclamations and orders that Lincoln issued. Habeas corpus is the name of a legal action, or writ, through which a person can seek relief from being unlawfully arrested and detained. The writ of habeas corpus safeguards an individual's freedom and protects citizens against arbitrary state action. Also known as "The Great Writ," a writ of habeas corpus demands that a prisoner be brought before the court, together with proof of authority, allowing the court to determine whether the law enforcement has lawful authority to hold that person. If not, the person should be released from custody. Lincoln's action was also motivated by requests from generals to set up military courts to arrest Copperheads and those in the Union who supported the Confederate cause. The suspension was challenged in court and overturned by the U.S. Circuit Court in Maryland, led by Supreme Court Chief Justice Roger B. Taney. Lincoln, however, ignored Taney's ruling.

On March 3, 1863, Congress passed the Habeas Corpus Act of 1863, giving Congress—and not the president—the power to suspend habeas corpus. This bill suspended habeas corpus across the nation and was passed to acknowledge Taney's ruling as well. In 1864, Lambdin P. Milligan and four others were accused of planning to steal Union weapons and invade Union prisoner-of-war camps. They were sentenced to hang by a military court. Their execution was not set until May 1865, however, so they were able to argue the case after the Civil War. The Supreme Court of the United States ruled it unconstitutional for the president to try to convict citizens before military tribunals when civil courts were functioning. The trial of civilians by military tribunals is allowed only if civilian courts are closed, and if the area is within an area of active military operations. This decision was one of the key Supreme Court cases of the American Civil War that dealt with wartime civil liberties and martial law.

PROCLAMATION OF AMNESTY AND RECONSTRUCTION

During the war, when much of Tennessee, Louisiana, and North Carolina had fallen to Union soldiers, Lincoln had appointed military governors to bring those states back into the Union. On December 8, 1863, the president issued a Proclamation of Amnesty (or pardons) and Reconstruction. Except for high military and civil officers of the Confederacy, the proclamation stated that all Southerners who took an oath of loyalty to the Constitution and swore to obey the wartime legislation and proclamation regarding slavery would be granted pardons. As soon as 10 percent of each state's 1860 electorate agreed to these rules, that state could write a new constitution, elect new state officials, and send members to Congress. This plan became the basis of later Reconstruction. Already at this time, Lincoln faced sharp criticism for his policies. Some members of Congress thought the proclamation was too lenient for the Rebels. They wanted to see the South punished for its actions. Also, Congress demanded protection of freed slaves, who would be in danger because of the violent anger of Southerners.

The Civil War had radically changed American society. African Americans were free, the federal government had more power, and a war-battered South needed to be completely rebuilt—both its cities and economy. Racial equality was unimaginable to Southern whites, especially aristocrats whose families had owned slaves for generations. Poor whites were also concerned about their future. They could not fathom having to compete with a freed slave for work. Any ideas to restructure the South sparked heated debate, opposition, criticism, and sometimes violence. Reconstruction of the South was like a second civil war. Lincoln, however, would not be a part of this stage. A young actor named John Wilkes Booth had other plans for the president.

ASSASSINATION

On April 11, 1865, from the White House steps, Lincoln delivered a speech about the war's end and hope for America's future. Standing in the crowd that night was John Wilkes Booth, a 26-year-old actor who was born in Maryland and held great passion for the South. When war broke out, Booth openly professed his loyalty to the Confederacy and his hatred of Lincoln. During the war, he even helped smuggle quinine and other needed medicines into the Confederacy. As his hatred festered, he devised a scheme to kidnap Lincoln and take him behind Confederate lines in Virginia, where he would be held hostage until thousands of Southern soldiers were released from Northern prisons.

This was not the first plot to kidnap or assassinate the president. As soon as he was elected in 1860, rumors of his assassination circled in the streets of many cities across the nation. "I long ago made up my mind that if anyone wants to kill me, he will do it," Lincoln once told a reporter. "If I wore a shirt of [armor], and kept myself surrounded by a bodyguard, it would

John Wilkes Booth was a member of a prominent family of actors from Maryland. Booth's hatred for Lincoln grew as the Confederacy's defeat became more certain, and his plan to kidnap Lincoln for ransom became a murder plot in an effort to throw the Union into a state of panic and confusion. After assassinating the president, there was little sympathy for him, and he later died of a gunshot wound to the neck.

be all the same. There are a thousand ways of getting at a man if it is desired that he should be killed."

In August of 1864, Booth built a team of conspirators. He recruited two of his boyhood chums from Baltimore to help with the plot—Samuel Arnold and Michael O'Laughlin. Planning to ferry the president across the Potomac River, he also enlisted the help of Prussian-born George Atzerodt from Port Tobacco, Maryland. Atzerodt had ferried Confederate spies across the river and knew all the creeks and inlets. Another ally, John Surratt, added firsthand knowledge of the Confederate underground that was active in southern Maryland. Surratt's mother, Mary—who may or may not have been privy to the plot—provided headquarters for the conspirators in the inn she owned in Surrattsvill, Maryland, and at the boardinghouse she opened on H Street in Washington. Booth also persuaded burly Lewis Paine, who had served the Confederate special ops group Mosby's Confederate Rangers, to be his hired thug. Finally, he invited into the scheme a young pharmacy clerk, David Herold, who was familiar with the poorly mapped roads below Washington. The group was loosely organized, tied together only by a mutual devotion to the Confederate cause.

Booth created several plans. His first scheme was to capture Lincoln while he was attending Ford's Theatre on January 18. Entering the presidential box, Booth would grab Lincoln, tie him up, lower him down to the stage, and then whisk him off to the Confederacy. The plan lacked practicality, however. There was no way he would be able to bind the powerful six-foot-four president, and even if he could, it was doubtful the audience would just let him carry Lincoln away. A second, more realistic plot was to capture the president while he was out riding in his carriage. But the opportunity had never presented itself.

During the fall and winter of 1864, Booth spent hours studying maps and exploring the roads in Charles County, Maryland, anticipating the day when he would drag Lincoln across the Potomac. The whole scheme had a dramatic, theatrical element

JOHN WILKES BOOTH

"Our country owed all her troubles to him, and God simply made me the instrument of his punishment."

John Wilkes Booth was the ninth child out of ten born to Junius and Mary Ann, stage actors from Great Britain. John Wilkes Booth had dreams that went beyond life on the farm where he was born. When Booth was 17 years old, in August 1855, he made his stage debut as the Earl of Richmond in Shakespeare's *Richard III*. He became increasingly popular with audiences and was called "the handsomest man in America." By the late 1850s, Booth was earning $20,000 a year.

He performed around the country, even appearing before President Abraham Lincoln at Ford's Theatre in the role of the villain Raphael in *The Marble Heart* in 1863. During this performance, the president and those that accompanied him sat in the same box where he was assassinated two years later.

In 1858, Booth took a job with the Richmond Theatre in Virginia. Living in the South, he became attached to the Southern people and their way of life. In a letter to his brother-in-law, he said:

"This country was formed for the white not for the black man. And looking upon African slavery from the same stand-point, as held by those noble framers of our Constitution, I for one, have ever considered it, one of the greatest blessings (both for themselves and us) that God ever bestowed upon a favored nation."

As the war shifted to the North's advantage, Booth became increasingly agitated and outspoken in his hatred of

Lincoln. Many historians believe that Booth became a spy for the Confederacy. Not only did he deliver smuggled medicine to the Rebel soldiers during the war, but when he stayed with his sister Asia in Philadelphia, she recalled how "strange men called late at night for whispered consultations." The Booth family was divided on the subject of slavery, and John often quarreled with his brother Edwin. On December 2, 1859, Booth attended the hanging of militant abolitionist John Brown. Booth bought a militia uniform from the Richmond Grays and stood guard at the foot of the scaffold while Brown was hanged. In the spring of 1862, Booth was arrested for making antigovernment remarks. By late summer of 1864, he began making plans to kidnap the president.

The last straw came when Lincoln delivered a speech after General Robert E. Lee surrendered to General Ulysses S. Grant in which he discussed granting voting rights to blacks. He and his coconspirators put their plan into effect, which went from a kidnapping to an assassination plot, and on April 14, 1865, Lincoln became the first president to be assassinated. Twelve days later, Booth was killed while hiding out in a barn with one of his co-conspirators, David Herold.

Following Booth's death, some writers developed theories that Booth escaped. One individual, Finis L. Bates claimed to have met Booth in Texas in the 1870s. In 1903, a man who resembled Booth committed suicide in Oklahoma. Bates claimed the body and toured around the country with it, displaying the body as a sideshow at local carnivals and wrote a book about it in 1907. Other books also have been written about a possible escape by Booth, but these claims were never proven. In the mid-1990s, a Baltimore circuit court judge blocked an attempt to exhume Booth's presumed remains.

to it, and no one knows how serious Booth really was about carrying it out at that time. Lincoln's address on April 11, however, triggered Booth's fantasy into action. Standing in the crowd outside the White House, he heard the president talk about suffrage for African Americans who were educated and who had served in the Union armies. While imagining freed slaves voting and becoming U.S. citizens, Booth boiled with hatred. He vowed that this speech would be Lincoln's last.

Of course, Lincoln knew nothing about Booth's kidnapping plot. When he awoke on April 14—five days after Lee's surrender—he felt happier than he had in years. At three that afternoon, he went for a carriage ride with Mary. As they drove about the city, Mary chuckled and said, "Dear husband, you almost startle me by your great cheerfulness."

"And well I may feel so, Mary," Lincoln replied. "I consider *this* day, the war, has come to a close." He added a promise. "We must *both*, be more cheerful in the future—between the war and the loss of our darling Willie—we have both, been very miserable."

Later on that evening, Abe decided to celebrate his cheerful new outlook by taking his wife to the theatre. By the time they arrived at Ford's Theatre, at about eight thirty, the performance had already begun. The play, "Our American Cousin", was a popular comedy, starring Laura Keene, about the American bumpkin Asa Trenchard who goes to England to claim a fortune he has inherited from a wealthy relative. He is pursued by a fortune-hunting Englishwoman, Mrs. Mountchessington, who wants him to marry her daughter, Augusta. When the president and his party—a young army major, Henry Rathbone, and his fiancée, Clara Harris—arrived, the play suddenly stopped and the orchestra burst into a chorus of "Hail to the Chief." The entire audience jumped up and cheered. The Lincolns climbed the stairs to the presidential box and took their seats. And the production resumed where it had left off. With Mary nestled close to Abe, the couple seemed to enjoy the play. The actors had taken the liberty, in places, to change the lines to add a bit of extra humor. In one scene, the frail heroine asked for a seat that was protected by the draft. The actor who played Lord Dundreary was supposed to reply, "Well, you're not the only one that wants to escape the draft." Instead, he said, "You are mistaken. The draft has already been stopped by order of the President." Familiar with the play, Abe caught the joke and let out a hearty laugh from his seat above the stage.

In the meantime, Booth had been hastily amending his scheme. He decided to murder Lincoln, as well as Vice President Andrew Johnson and Secretary of State William Seward. By wiping out these posts, the nation would have to run a new election, giving the former Confederacy a chance to take over. In the moment of truth, however, Booth had trouble convincing his coconspirators to go along with the assassination. Originally, they had agreed to abduct the president, not murder him. His followers dwindled down to two loyal accomplices: Herold and Paine. On Friday afternoon, April 14, Booth learned that Lincoln would be at Ford's Theatre that night. He decided this was his golden opportunity. Paine and Herold fanned out to find their targets—Seward and Johnson, leaving Booth to murder the president alone. All three assassinations were to take place simultaneously, at ten fifteen that night.

As a celebrated actor, Booth had no trouble slipping upstairs and into the presidential box. He snuck up behind Lincoln, who was hunched forward with his chin in his hand. Booth stretched out his arm, aimed his derringer pistol at the back of Lincoln's head, and pulled the trigger. Lincoln slumped forward, and Mary reached out to catch him. Immediately, Major Rathbone tried to seize the assassin. Booth pulled out a razor-sharp hunting knife and lunged at Rathbone, cutting his arm to the bone. Then, Booth pushed his victim aside and vaulted out of the box onto the stage, 12 feet below. On his way down, he snagged his heel on the swags decorating the box. He landed awkwardly onstage, breaking his shin bone. As he staggered backstage, he shouted, "Sic semper tyrannis!" ("Thus always to tyrants"—Viriginia's state motto.)

Up until this point, the audience was confused about what had just happened. Many of them thought it was part of the act. Then they heard the shrieking voice of Mary Lincoln echo through the theatre, "They have shot the President!" The audience looked up and saw the silver-blue smoke drifting out of the presidential box, so slowly it almost seemed like an eerie dream.

Any doctors there that night rushed to the president's side. They moved him out of the crowded theatre across Tenth Street to a house owned by William Petersen, a merchant tailor. Inside, they quickly carried him to a narrow bedroom at the rear of the first floor. Because Lincoln was so tall, the mattress was too short for him, and he had to be laid diagonally on the bed. For the next nine hours, he lay motionless, yet breathing, in the somber room, his family at his bedside. The bullet had entered his skull above his left ear and lodged behind his right eye. He never regained consciousness.

As dawn broke on the morning of April 15, Lincoln's breath grew fainter and fainter. At seven twenty-two, he died. Silence filled the small, crowded room. Young Robert, Lincoln's oldest son, then broke the stillness with overpowering sobs. Secretary of War and Lincoln's close friend, Edwin McMasters Stanton, stood at the foot of the bed, his face wet with tears. He slowly extended his right arm in an honored salute, raised his hat and placed it on his head, and then removed it. He solemnly stated, "Now he belongs to the ages."

Elsewhere, Paine had attacked his target, Secretary of State Seward. He had burst into Seward's house, stabbing him several times ruthlessly and leaving him bleeding and barely alive. On the other hand, Atzerodt became weakhearted and could not carry out his orders. He was picked up aimlessly wandering the city. By morning, Paine had also been arrested. But Booth had escaped on horseback. His crime did not go unpunished,

Although President Lincoln died on April 15, 1865, his body did not reach its final resting place of Springfield until May 4. In between, his body lay in state in the East Room of the White House, and then traveled by train along a winding route from Washington, D.C., through 442 communities in 9 states, the route in reverse of Lincoln's whistle-stop tour before his inauguration. Pictured is Lincoln's funeral procession down Pennsylvania Avenue, April 19, 1865.

however. On April 26, Stanton's men traced Booth to a farm in northern Virginia. There, finding him hiding in the barn, they shot and killed him.

On April 19, four days after his death, Lincoln's funeral was held in the East Room of the White House. Afterwards, a detachment of African-American troops led the long funeral procession up Pennsylvania Avenue. The procession slowly moved down the street toward the Capitol to the gentle roll of drums and the deep toll of church bells. Two days later, a funeral train carried Abraham Lincoln back to his hometown of Springfield, traveling through 180 cities and 7 states. At each stop, mourners paid their last respects to their fallen president. His body was laid to rest at Oak Ridge Cemetery.

Abraham Lincoln served the Union at one of the most difficult times in American history. Despite criticism and opposition, he triumphantly led the nation past a war that could have drastically altered the future of the United States. He successfully accomplished what he believed was his ultimate duty and responsibility—preserving the Union. His vision of freedom for all serves as a model of American policy still today.

CHRONOLOGY

1809   **February 12** Lincoln is born in a one-room log cabin on Nolin Creek in Kentucky to Thomas and Nancy.

1811   Lincoln family moves to 230-acre farm on Knob Creek near Sinking Spring.

1816   Lincoln family moves to the backwoods of Indiana.

1830   Lincolns make 200-mile journey to Illinois.

1831   Abraham takes a second flatboat trip to New Orleans; settles in New Salem.

1834   Lincoln elected to Illinois General Assembly and serves until 1842.

1837   Lincoln moves to Springfield and becomes a law partner of John T. Stuart.

1842   Marries Mary Todd on November 4.

1843   Unsuccessfully runs for U.S. Congress; son Robert Todd born on August 1.

1846   Second son Edward Baker born on March 10.

1850   Edward dies on February 1; William "Willie" Wallace born on December 21.

1853   Son Thomas "Tad" born on April 4.

1860   Elected the sixteenth president of the United States on November 6; seven states secede from the Union and form the Confederate States of America.

1861   Confederates open fire on Union troops at Fort Sumter on April 12; the Civil War begins; four more states secede from Union creating an eleven-state Confederacy; Union suffers a defeat at the first Battle of Bull Run.

1862   Willie dies of typhoid fever on February 20 at age 11; Confederate victory at the second Battle of Bull Run; the Battle of Antietam on September 17 becomes the bloodiest day in U.S. military history with 26,000 soldiers either dead, wounded, or missing.

1863   President Lincoln issues the Emancipation Proclamation, freeing all slaves in Rebel states on January 1; Union suffers another defeat at the Battle of Chancellorsville on May 1-4; Union wins a crucial victory at the Battle of Gettysburg on July 3.

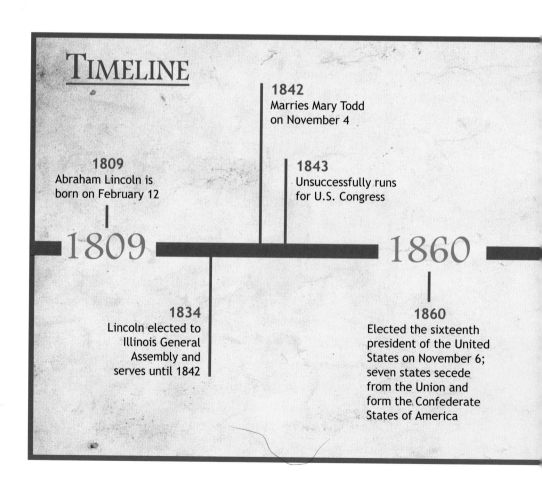

TIMELINE

1842
Marries Mary Todd
on November 4

1809
Abraham Lincoln is
born on February 12

1843
Unsuccessfully runs
for U.S. Congress

1809   1860

1834
Lincoln elected to
Illinois General
Assembly and
serves until 1842

1860
Elected the sixteenth
president of the United
States on November 6;
seven states secede
from the Union and
form the Confederate
States of America

1864   Sherman's army captures Atlanta on September 2
       and begins his 60-mile March to the Sea; Lincoln
       reelected on November 8;

1865   Confederate general Robert E. Lee surrenders his
       army to General Ulysses S. Grant at Appomattox
       Court House, Virginia, on April 9; Lincoln shot by
       John Wilkes Booth at Ford's Theatre on April 14; the
       president dies at 7:22 on the morning of April 15;
       Andrew Johnson becomes the seventeenth president
       of the United States; Booth is shot and killed at a

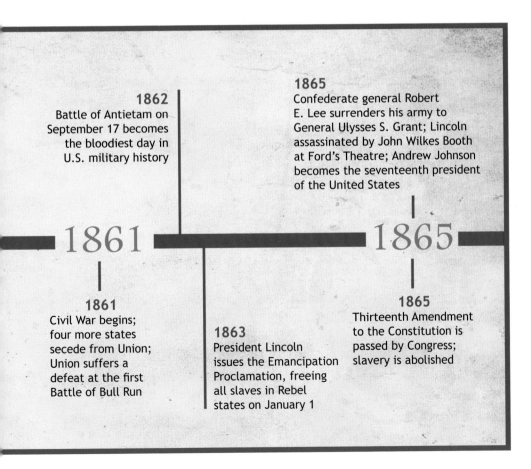

1862
Battle of Antietam on September 17 becomes the bloodiest day in U.S. military history

1865
Confederate general Robert E. Lee surrenders his army to General Ulysses S. Grant; Lincoln assassinated by John Wilkes Booth at Ford's Theatre; Andrew Johnson becomes the seventeenth president of the United States

1861   1865

1861
Civil War begins; four more states secede from Union; Union suffers a defeat at the first Battle of Bull Run

1863
President Lincoln issues the Emancipation Proclamation, freeing all slaves in Rebel states on January 1

1865
Thirteenth Amendment to the Constitution is passed by Congress; slavery is abolished

Virginia tobacco barn on April 26; Lincoln's body is laid to rest in Oak Ridge Cemetery outside of Springfield, Illinois; The Thirteenth Amendment to the Constitution is passed by Congress on December 6; slavery is abolished.

GLOSSARY

abolitionist   Someone who opposes slavery and works to end it.

campaign   A plan for a candidate who is running for election; also, a series of military operations designed to reach a single goal.

constable   A police officer in a small town.

docket   A list of cases to be tried by a court of law.

duties   Taxes on imports.

emancipation   The act of setting someone free.

ferry   To take people across a river; also, the boat used to do so.

flank   The left or right side of a military formation.

ironclad   Covered with iron plating for protection; term used to describe certain ships used in the Civil War.

litigation   A lawsuit.

magistrate   A justice of the peace.

martial law   Rule by military authorities.

menial   Word used to describe petty tasks.

Northwest Ordinance   An act of Congress that opened up vast territories of western land for settlement.

platform   A statement of policy made by a candidate during an election.

Reconstruction   The era after the Civil War during which the South was rebuilt.

secede   To withdraw.

suffrage   The right to vote.

BIBLIOGRAPHY

"Abraham Lincoln," Microsoft Encarta Online Encyclopedia 2008. Available online at http://encarta.msn.com/encyclopedia_761577113/Abraham_Lincoln.html.

Barton, William Eleazar. *The Life of Abraham Lincoln*. Brooklyn, N.Y.: Bobbs-Merrill, 1925.

Canby, Courtlandt. *Lincoln and the Civil War: a Profile and a History*. New York: G. Braziller, 1960.

Donald, David Herbert. *Lincoln*. New York: Touchstone, 1996.

———. *We Are Lincoln Men*. New York: Simon & Schuster, 2003.

Fans of Fieger. "Lawyer Hall of Fame." Available online at http://fansoffieger.com/lincoln.htm.

Fenster, J.M. *The Case of Abraham Lincoln*. New York: Palgrave Macmillan, 2007.

Freedman, Russell. *Lincoln: A Photobiography*. New York: Clarion Books, 1987.

Lincoln, Abraham. *The Collected Works of Abraham Lincoln*. New Brunswick, N.J.: Rutgers University Press, 1955.

Plowden, David. *Lincoln and His America, 1809–1865*. New York: Viking Press, 1970.

Sandburg, Carl. *Abraham Lincoln: The Prairie Years and the War Years*. New York: Harcourt Brace Jovanovich, 1954.

FURTHER RESOURCES

BOOKS

Aretha, David. *Jefferson Davis*. New York: Chelsea House Publishers, 2008.

Crompton, Samuel Willard. *Ulysses S. Grant*. New York: Chelsea House Publishers, 2008.

Graves, Kerry. *The Civil War*. Mankato, Minn.: Capstone Press, 2001.

Hyslop, Steve. *Eyewitness to the Civil War*. Washington, D.C.: National Geographic, 2006.

Koestler-Grack, Rachel A. *Stonewall Jackson*. New York: Chelsea House Publishers, 2008.

———. *William Tecumseh Sherman*. New York: Chelsea House Publishers, 2008.

McNeese, Tim. *The Abolitionist Movement: Ending Slavery*. New York: Chelsea House Publishers, 2007.

———. *The Emancipation Proclamation: Ending Slavery in America*. New York: Chelsea House Publishers, 2008.

———. *Robert E. Lee*. New York: Chelsea House Publishers, 2008.

Ray, Delia. *Behind the Blue & Gray: The Soldier's Life in the Civil War*. New York: Lodestar Books, 1991.

Sonneborn, Liz. *Harriet Beecher Stowe*. New York: Chelsea House Publishers, 2008.

Sterngass, Jon. *John Brown*. New York: Chelsea House Publishers, 2008.

Wagner, Heather Lehr. *The Outbreak of the Civil War: A Nation Tears Apart*. New York: Chelsea House Publishers, 2008.

WEB SITES

Abraham Lincoln Research Site
http://members.aol.com/RVSNorton/Lincoln2.html

CivilWar.com: the Home of the Civil War
http://www.civilwar.com

The Civil War at PBS
http://www.pbs.org/civilwar

Slavery and the Making of America
http://www.pbs.org/wnet/slavery

PICTURE CREDITS

✂ INDEX ✂

ABOUT THE AUTHOR

RACHEL A. KOESTLER-GRACK has worked with nonfiction books as an editor and writer since 1999. During her career, she has worked extensively with historical topics, ranging from the Middle Ages to the colonial era to the civil rights movement. In addition, she has written numerous biographies on a variety of historical and contemporary figures. Rachel lives with her husband and daughter in the German community of New Ulm, Minnesota.